ISSUE 14, FEBRUARY 2022

AUSTRALIAN FOF

G000166275

Contributors

Yu-Jie Chen is an assistant research professor at Academia Sinica and an affiliated scholar at the US–Asia Law Institute of NYU.

Stephen Dziedzic is the ABC's Foreign Affairs (Asia Pacific) reporter.

Linda Jakobson founded China Matters, a public policy initiative.

Lynne O'Donnell was bureau chief for Associated Press and AFP in Afghanistan between 2009 and 2017.

William A. Stoltz is Senior Adviser for Public Policy at the National Security College at the Australian National University.

Cait Storr is Chancellor's Postdoctoral Research Fellow in law at the University of Technology, Sydney.

Brendan Taylor is a professor of strategic studies at the Australian National University.

Andrew Wear is a policy expert and author.

Hugh White is an emeritus professor of strategic studies at the Australian National University.

Australian Foreign Affairs is published three times a year by Schwartz Books Pty Ltd. Publisher: Morry Schwartz. ISBN 978-1-76064-3454 ISSN 2208-5912 ALL RIGHTS RESERVED. No part of this publication may be reproduced, stored in a retrieval system, or transmitted in any form by any means, electronic, mechanical, photocopying, recording or otherwise, without the prior consent of the publishers. Essays, reviews and correspondence © retained by the authors. Subscriptions – 1 year print & digital auto-renew (3 issues): $49.99 within Australia incl. GST. 1 year print and digital subscription (3 issues): $59.99 within Australia incl. GST. 2 year print & digital (6 issues): $114.99 within Australia incl. GST. 1 year digital only auto-renew: $29.99. Payment may be made by MasterCard, Visa or Amex, or by cheque made out to Schwartz Books Pty Ltd. Payment includes postage and handling. To subscribe, fill out the form inside this issue, subscribe online at www.australianforeignaffairs.com, email subscribe@australianforeignaffairs.com or phone 1800 077 514 / 61 3 9486 0288. Correspondence should be addressed to: The Editor, Australian Foreign Affairs, 22–24 Northumberland Street, Collingwood, VIC, 3066 Australia Phone: 61 3 9486 0288 / Fax: 61 3 9486 0244 Email: enquiries@australianforeignaffairs. com Editor: Jonathan Pearlman. Deputy Editor: Kirstie Innes-Will. Associate Editor: Chris Feik. Consulting Editor: Allan Gyngell. Digital Editor and Marketing: Georgia Mill. Management: Elisabeth Young. Subscriptions: Iryna Byelyayeva and Sam Perazzo. Publicity: Anna Lensky. Design: Peter Long. Production Coordination: Marilyn de Castro. Typesetting: Tristan Main. Cover photograph: Mykhailo Polenok / Alamy Stock Photo. Printed in Australia by McPherson's Printing Group.

Editor's Note

THE TAIWAN CHOICE

For decades, Australia's approach to Taiwan has been based on a convenient diplomatic contortion. Australia does not recognise Taiwan as a state, but also does not explicitly say it is part of China; nor, until late 2021, did Australia signal whether it was committed to defending Taiwan from invasion.

Australia's awkward Taiwan policy is prone to being misinterpreted and to eliciting gaffes from leaders who try to explain it. Last May, for instance, Australian prime minister Scott Morrison was asked in a morning radio interview about his position on Taiwan's calls for countries to support it against Chinese president Xi Jinping's "expansionism".

"I don't wish to add to any uncertainty," Morrison said, before confusingly – and incorrectly – saying Australia supported the "one country, two systems" formula – a policy originally designed by Beijing to persuade Taiwan to integrate. But Morrison was not suddenly adopting a new pro-China approach; most likely, he confused Australia's "one country" position on Hong Kong with its "one China" policy on Taiwan. The mistake highlighted the difficulty of presenting a straightforward account of a policy that strives for ambiguity.

Australia's current policy is designed to preserve the political status quo – in which a thriving Taiwan is free of China's control – and to ensure that Canberra does not need to formally commit to militarily protect Taiwan.

The most significant example of Australia's struggle to uphold its Taiwan ambiguity occurred in 2004, when, during a visit to Beijing, the foreign minister, Alexander Downer said that the ANZUS Treaty would not require Australia to automatically support the United States in a war over Taiwan. Asked to clarify Downer's comments, Australian prime minister John Howard said there was no need to "get into a political science lecture" or to confirm Australia's commitments in the event of such a war. "The issue of conflict between China and the United States is hypothetical," he said. "Our policy is to be friendly with both."

But the difficulty for Australia is that the prospect of war is no longer so hypothetical. Xi has pledged to achieve "reunification" with Taiwan and is equipping the Chinese military for a potential takeover; Taiwan says it will resist; and Washington is backing Taiwan. It cannot be said that Australia, which has been subject to trade sanctions and a diplomatic freeze by China, is still "friendly with both".

Some Australian politicians have begun calling for Canberra to dispense with the ambiguity and explicitly commit to defending Taiwan. Notably, Defence Minister Peter Dutton declared in November 2021 that Australia would inevitably back the US in a war over Taiwan, saying "there is no sense sticking your head in the sand".

Morrison did not repeat Dutton's comments, but insisted he supported them. "This is not a time where Australia can afford people having an each-way bet on national security," Morrison said. It was an odd way to present a change to one of Australia's most important foreign policies.

If Australia is going to dispense with its each-way bet on Taiwan, it needs to grasp the risks and ramifications. A war would reshape Asia – it would determine the future role of the US in the region, and it would shake the foundations of the US alliance, which has been the bedrock of Australian security since World War II.

As tensions rise in the Taiwan Strait, Australia's position of ambiguity is becoming harder to preserve or explain. As Australia weighs its choices, it must understand the prospects of a war, the likely outcome and the potential consequences – for China, the US, the Asia-Pacific region, and Taiwan.

Jonathan Pearlman

REALITY CHECK

Taiwan cannot be defended

Hugh White

It is not inevitable that America and China will go to war over Taiwan, but the risk is real, and growing. If it comes, this war would be unlike anything we have seen for seventy-five years, and quite possibly unlike any war ever seen before. It would be the first conflict between major world powers since 1950, when China and America fought in Korea. It would also be the first serious war between nuclear-armed powers. Until now, there have only been minor border clashes between nuclear adversaries – Pakistan and India, India and China, and China and the Soviets. A war over Taiwan would be nothing like these. We must expect that once fighting began, it would swiftly escalate into a full-scale regional conflict, and nuclear war would then become hard to avoid. The consequences for America, for China, for the people of Taiwan and for everyone else in Asia and beyond would be immense, and disastrous. And yet no one seems to be seriously trying to reduce the risk of this war happening.

In fact, America and China, the key players, both seem content to allow the tensions around Taiwan to build. Neither side wants to go to war, but both sides think that the possibility of a clash will serve their wider strategic aims. Washington hopes that the threat of war will deter China from challenging America's primacy in East Asia, and Beijing hopes that it will deter America from trying to contain China's ambitions. It is a very dangerous game.

It is a game as old as power politics. When great powers compete, a relatively modest issue acquires outsized importance as the focus of their rivalry and the test of their strength and resolve. This is how the Thucydides Trap is set. In 433 BCE, the fate of a minor colony on Corfu became the test of whether Athens or Sparta would dominate the Greek world. In 1914, Austria's right to punish Serbia for the Archduke's assassination became the test of the entire European strategic order. In 1938, the Sudetenland became a test of the Western allies' resolve to stop Hitler, and in 1939, the status of Danzig and the Polish Corridor became another. In 1949, the fate of West Berlin became the test of US resolve to contain the Soviet Union. And today, the future of Taiwan has, it seems, became the test of whether China or America dominates East Asia in the decades to come, and whether the post–Cold War vision of US global leadership can endure.

Taiwan's role in this escalating rivalry is not surprising. It has been the most sensitive issue in US–China relations ever since America "lost" China to the communists in 1949. Beijing has since then seen the assertion of its sovereignty over Taiwan and its right to take control of it – by force if necessary – as fundamental to its place as a power in Asia. And America has seen its capacity to deny Taiwan to Beijing the same way. In the 1970s, awkward compromises were reached to reconcile these inherently incompatible positions and allow the US–China relationship to flourish. Those compromises, which have framed Taiwan's unique international status for the past forty years, were sustainable as long as both sides were determined to make the relationship work. That is no longer true, and the compromises are coming apart.

The precarious status quo over Taiwan is under pressure from developments both within Taiwan and beyond it. Since Taiwan's transition to democracy in the 1990s, it has become less and less likely that its people will ever willingly agree to be brought under Beijing's control, as Beijing has long hoped. This has become especially clear in the past five years, since the election of President Tsai Ing-wen. Under her predecessor, Ma Ying-jeou, it seemed possible that as China grew richer and – as many expected – less authoritarian, the people of Taiwan would come round to the idea of unification. But Tsai's successive election wins, based on little more than her anti-Beijing credentials, have confirmed that the opposite is happening. The Taiwanese have become more opposed to unification as China becomes more authoritarian, especially since Beijing has clamped down on Hong Kong. This must raise fears in Zhongnanhai that the time for patience is past, and that unification needs to be achieved sooner rather later. At the same time, Taiwan's vibrant democracy makes it harder for Washington to stick to the limits on interactions with Taipei that were agreed on forty years ago, when Taiwan, too, was a dictatorship, and increases the pressure to shield Taiwan from Chinese oppression.

The impact of these trends on Taiwan's predicament is greatly amplified by the escalating strategic contest between America and China. This contest is often characterised as concerning issues such as freedom of navigation or respect for international law, but it is much bigger than that. It is a contest between the world's two strongest states over which of them will lead the globe's most dynamic and prosperous region in the decades ahead. America wants to preserve the dominant position it has held and successfully defended for over a century. China wants America to withdraw from East Asia so it can

When the next Taiwan crisis flares, both sides will face a deadly threat and a golden opportunity

take its place as the region's primary power and at least the equal to any power globally. For both countries, the outcome is fundamental to their identities as nations. The stakes are therefore high. Great powers do not go to war with one another lightly, but these are the kind of stakes for which, throughout history, they have done so. If America and China go to war over Taiwan, it won't really be about Taiwan, any more than the First World War was about Austria's right to punish Serbia. It will be about the shape of the future regional and global order.

Tests of resolve

To understand the likelihood of a war over Taiwan, we need to understand how Washington and Beijing use the possibility of war in their contest for leadership. Leadership in an international system is largely built on perceptions. A country is treated as a leader if it is perceived as such. Many factors contribute to building and maintaining perceptions of leadership, including economic reach, diplomatic weight and the social, cultural and ideological qualities often labelled "soft power". But the deepest foundation of leadership is the perceived willingness and capacity of a country to use force to assert its will. That is what both attracts followers and deters adversaries.

America's leadership in Asia over many decades has been founded on the perception among Asian nations that it is willing and able to use force to protect its friends and punish its enemies – even against other great powers. Above all, its leadership has been based on the unwillingness of either Japan or China, as the region's strongest states, to risk a war with it, instead accepting subservient places in the regional order. The need to preserve such perceptions is the reason that America has invested so heavily in the kind of high-level forces that would only be needed in a major-power war.

This makes China's task clear. To undermine US leadership and assert its primacy in East Asia, Beijing must change perceptions in the region about America's capacity and resolve to fight and win a war with China. Beijing must show that as its power has grown, the balance of strength and resolve has shifted its way – that it is willing and able to fight America in East Asia, and America is not willing to fight China. America's task is equally clear. To preserve its leadership, it must show that America, not China, is willing to fight.

Both sides see Taiwan as the issue over which their resolve will be tested. America wants to compel Beijing to accept that Taiwan's status will need to evolve in ways that increasingly resemble full independence. China wants to show that America is no longer willing or able to prevent China taking control of Taiwan – by force if necessary.

It is not the first or the only issue the two powers have used to test one another. Since 2012, the South China Sea has been the focus of a preliminary round in the contest. By defying Washington's loud protests, China's provocative actions there have tested America's willingness to defend the principles of international order it accuses China of violating. But any action with a real chance of forcing China to stop doing things like building island bases risks a clash that might escalate into a war, and Washington has not been willing to take that risk. China has won that round.

Now, as their rivalry grows, the contest moves to Taiwan, a clearer and more dangerous test. It was always a little hard to believe that either America or China would really risk a war over the rocks and reefs of the South China Sea. But Taiwan is different: both sides have long asserted their willingness to go to war over it, even when the relationship has been at its warmest. To repeat, neither side wants a war. They both hope to win the contest by forcing the other side to back off, thus destroying their rival's leadership credentials.

When the next Taiwan crisis flares, both sides will face a deadly threat and a golden opportunity. If America abandons Taiwan to avoid war, then its strategic credibility in Asia will be destroyed. Washington has always made it crystal clear that behind the artificial ambiguities of its One China policy lies a commitment to defend Taiwan – a commitment as strong as the one to its formal allies in Asia. If Washington now decides that the cost of defending Taiwan against today's powerful China is too high, those allies – Japan, South Korea, the Philippines, even Australia – would naturally, and rightly, doubt America's willingness to defend them either. Non-allies like Indonesia and Vietnam will be even less inclined to rely on US support. Countries across the region would have less reason to side with America, and more reason to deal with China as best they can. That is how strategic leadership shifts. The US alliance system, and its position as an Asian power, would crumble. China would take its place. Conversely, if China backed off, its claim to America's position in Asia would collapse, and US leadership would be resoundingly affirmed – at least for a while. The communist government in Beijing would suffer a devastating blow to its standing, and perhaps even to its domestic legitimacy.

So as the next Taiwan crisis unfolds, both sides will have a big incentive to talk and act as if they are prepared to fight, hoping and expecting that this will deliver them a costless victory by making the other side back down. But there is a fair chance that they will both be wrong about this, in which case the crisis will keep escalating. Then both will face a disastrous choice between humiliation and war. In such situations, leaders in the past have often chosen war. This is how wars happen despite neither side wanting or intending them.

China's choices

How likely are we to face this kind of scenario? That probably depends most on China. As the ambitious nation, it is more likely to initiate a test of power and resolve by moving militarily against Taiwan. The temptation for Xi Jinping and his colleagues must be great, because success would decisively accomplish "the great rejuvenation of the Chinese nation", restore China's place as the leading regional power and humiliate its rival. It would be a crowning achievement for Xi himself. Taiwan's own defences would pose little deterrent. Nor would the

The only option would be to consider nuclear weapons

significant but not insuperable challenge of subduing Taiwanese resistance to Beijing's rule once the island had been seized. But the idea of war with America must give China pause. That is probably the decisive consideration currently weighing against seizing Taiwan.

This has not always been the case. For a long time, Beijing plainly judged the economic and diplomatic costs of trying to seize Taiwan to be unacceptable. Economically, a breach with Washington over Taiwan would disrupt or destroy access to the US and wider global markets, capital and technology that have been essential to China's growth, and hence to everything the Chinese Communist Party has been trying to achieve. A threat to that relationship was therefore unthinkable. Diplomatically, China still had a lot to lose by direct confrontation with an America that remained unquestionably the world's leading power. But much has changed in twenty-five years, and especially in the last five years. The economic and technological relationship with America is now less important to China, and has anyway been seriously disrupted. Though an economic breach with Washington would be hugely costly, it is no longer unthinkable. Today, Beijing can be a lot more confident of its ability to manage the diplomatic fallout of a move against Taiwan, as its global position has strengthened with its economic weight, while America's has been weakened by erratic leadership and strategic failure.

That leaves the military deterrent. At the turn of the century, a maritime war with America over Taiwan would have led to a certain, swift and humiliating Chinese defeat. But the military balance in the Western Pacific between America and China has shifted. The leaders in Beijing may well believe that they would now win a maritime war over Taiwan. They probably also believe that their counterparts in Washington think that too. If so, the balance of deterrence may have swung in China's favour, meaning that America, when push came to shove, would decide not to fight for Taiwan. A move against Taiwan must then seem very tempting indeed. They would not deliberately seek a war with America, but they might be willing to gamble that America would not fight.

Much therefore depends on how Xi and his colleagues assess Washington's resolve. That, in turn, depends on how they think a decision over whether to fight for Taiwan would look to Washington – what is really at stake for America, and is it worth a long and costly war?

America's weakening deterrence

What kind of war would it be? There is no reason to hope that a US–China conflict over Taiwan would be limited to "grey zone" clashes or cyberattacks. Both sides have massive air and naval forces, and would need to be willing to commit them or forfeit the contest. That is why any sustained clash is likely to escalate into a full-scale regional maritime war. China cannot match America's capacity to project power globally, but in the Western Pacific it has the advantage of location, and has developed capable anti-access/area denial (A2/AD) forces to exploit this advantage. America, on the other hand, must project force into the area of operations around Taiwan from distant bases. America would be unable to match the scale of airpower that China could sustain in the area, and its forces would be vulnerable to Chinese air defences. America's few bases in the region would be subject to Chinese missile attack, and its ships would face formidable threats from China's impressive range of anti-ship systems.

These judgements are no longer seriously disputed. Many US assessments, both official and independent, conclude that China would now take a heavy toll on US ships and aircraft approaching China or Taiwan. In the first days and weeks of a war, America must expect, for example, to lose any or all of the aircraft carriers it sends into battle. Worse, there is no reason to expect that these losses would be counterbalanced by decisive strategic success. War is always uncertain, but the most likely outcome of a war over Taiwan is clear. US forces would inflict heavy losses on China, but they would not be enough to secure control of the maritime battlespace, nor would they be enough to force China to yield. After a few weeks of heavy losses, America would be no closer to victory, and instead face a costly and inconclusive stalemate. The support of US allies, if they chose to join the fight, would make no material difference to the likely outcome.

What, then, could America do to break the stalemate? It cannot seize and hold substantial Chinese mainland territory, let alone occupy the entire country. No conventional bombing campaign could compel surrender, as World War II and Vietnam showed. Trade blockades have never worked against a continental-scale power like China. And no one, surely, would imagine that American attacks would inspire the Chinese people to topple their government on Washington's behalf.

So the only option would be to consider nuclear weapons. America has always been willing to threaten their use if its conventional forces fail. This "first use" doctrine, dating from the Cold War, has been much debated but never repealed, and now assumes great significance in East Asia. The harder it becomes to win a conventional war with China, the more Washington must rely on nuclear threats to prevail. No one intends to actually use nuclear weapons, of course. Instead, they hope and expect that merely threatening nuclear attack would convince

China to yield. It is not an unreasonable expectation. As long as the Chinese believe America's threats, this is probably the way – the only way – to win a war over Taiwan.

But that path to victory is far from certain because China has nuclear weapons too. Its arsenal is designed specifically to counter this kind of nuclear blackmail. China has many fewer nuclear weapons than America, but it has enough to target a dozen or more US cities, and the United States has no reliable way of ensuring that some of them do not reach their targets and kill hundreds of thousands of Americans. Beijing evidently thinks this is enough to deter any US president from ordering a nuclear attack, and to frustrate Washington's hopes of using nuclear threats to force it to yield.

All this suggests that America's deterrence of China is weak

Are they right? That is a complex question with no clear answers. Perhaps America could deter a Chinese retaliatory strike with the threat of counter-retaliation, thus restoring the credibility of the original threat. But China might in turn threaten counter-counter-retaliation. The reality is that no one knows who might win this deadly game. Nor do they know whether one or both sides might circumvent the cycle of threat and counter-threat by deciding to launch a nuclear strike and accept the consequent retaliation. What we do know is that neither side could go to war without weighing the very real danger that it might become a nuclear war, in which their cities and populations would be targets. We also know that this danger would weigh on American leaders more heavily than on Chinese leaders, for two reasons.

First, China has a better chance of achieving its objective of taking Taiwan without threatening nuclear war than America does of stopping it. So America would probably have to make the first move towards the nuclear threshold – and without much confidence that even this would achieve its objectives. Any sane president would baulk at making that choice, and probably baulk at starting a war that might so easily force them to confront it. Second, China's stake is higher than America's. It is not just that Taiwan is more important to China than it is to America. The wider prize of strategic primacy in East Asia also matters more to China than it does to America, for the simple reason that it is China's backyard, not America's. The Americans should know that, and they should know the Chinese know it too. That gives the Chinese a big advantage in a deadly game of nuclear bluff and counter-bluff. The sobering conclusion is that America cannot rely on nuclear threats to break a conventional stalemate and win a war with China, and that means it cannot expect to prevail in a test of arms over Taiwan.

Americans should understand all this, but they might not. People in Washington, including President Biden and his team, sometimes talk as if they think failure to defend Taiwan would pose a threat not just to America's leadership in East Asia, but to America itself – in the same way Washington was convinced throughout the Cold War that defending Berlin was essential to protecting America from Soviet domination. If they really think this way about Taiwan, then they would be willing to fight a nuclear war to defend it, as they were over Berlin, and the Chinese had better take note. But do Americans think that, and do the Chinese believe they do? It seems unlikely, for two reasons.

The first is that China does not pose the same kind of threat to America as the Soviets did at the height of the Cold War. Although China today is far stronger relative to the United States than the Soviets ever were, it does not have the potential to dominate Eurasia that the Soviets once had. In the 1950s, India, China and Western Europe were all far weaker than the Soviet Union, and there was a real risk that, without US containment, Moscow could establish hegemony over the whole of Eurasia. For all its strength, present-day China has no chance of doing that because its neighbours are too strong. A China that takes Taiwan and dominates East Asia would still not dominate Eurasia, or be able to threaten America directly.

The second is that, for all the talk of a "new Cold War", America is not behaving as if it is nearly as serious about containing China as it was about containing the Soviet Union. That is not just because of the obvious appeal of Donald Trump's "America First" isolationism and the corresponding "Foreign Policy for the Middle Class" isola-tionism of the Biden administration, reflected in the withdrawal from Afghanistan. It is also evident in Washington's failure, under both Republican and Democratic administrations, to back the tough talk of strategic rivalry with concrete action that imposes genuine con-straints on China's freedom of action. Diplomatic talk shops like the Quad don't cut it, and the fact that Washington seems to take the

Quad so seriously will only help to convince Beijing how unserious Washington really is. The underlying problem is that Washington's foreign policy establishment has talked up America's determination to confront and contain China without properly considering, or explaining to the American people, how that can be done, how much it will cost and whether the cost is justified. No one has properly explained that it might mean nuclear war. A crisis over Taiwan would make the immense costs and risks inescapably clear, prompting a more sober consideration of America's real interests and objectives. Chinese leaders might well judge that, when that happens, the Americans will not choose to start a war over Taiwan that they probably cannot win, and in which they might lose American cities.

All this suggests that America's deterrence of China is weak. There is a real danger that the Chinese leadership comes to believe that America would not fight to defend Taiwan, and decides to go ahead and use force to seize it. It would be a gamble, of course, and China's leaders are not reckless. But they are clearly ambitious, and impatient to assert China's power and position. It is hard to see how else they can bring the present strategic rivalry with America to a head, and they already seem willing to run risks in order to do so. No one would really be surprised if they decide to roll the dice. There would then be just two possibilities. Either their gamble pays off and America does not fight, in which case the US era in East Asia is at an end and a new era of Chinese leadership begins. Or they are wrong, and America and China go to war. If that happens, Canberra will get a call.

Australia's uncomfortable options

If America goes to war with China over Taiwan, Washington will expect Australia to fully commit to the fight. Whatever the lawyers and historians might say about the precise scope of Australia's formal obligations under the ANZUS Treaty, the strategic and political reality is that our major ally would not be satisfied with the kind of modest, cautious contributions we have so often provided to US-led coalitions in the Middle East. Washington would expect us to send all the forces we had, for whatever tasks the Pentagon wanted them for.

This would pose one of the hardest strategic choices any Australian government has ever faced, comparable only with the decisions to go to war in 1914 and 1939. The stakes for Australia would be as large as they

> **Quite soon – probably within a decade – America's era as a major strategic player in East Asia will have passed**

were in those earlier crises – the survival of the international system in Asia and beyond on which we have depended for our prosperity and security. But this choice might be harder than either of those, because the chances are lower that we would be on the winning side and would achieve our aim of sustaining the status quo. That is because neither we nor our allies have ever faced an adversary in Asia as powerful as China is today.

Nonetheless, it seems clear that Canberra would readily agree. Most political leaders and government officials would say that "we have no choice". They'd say that Australia's only hope to avoid falling under Chinese hegemony is for America to successfully contain it, and Australia must therefore do literally all it can to help America prevail. And they'd say that Australia's standing as a US ally, and indeed the survival of the alliance itself, would be fatally endangered if Australia failed to meet America's expectations in this most severe test.

Canberra's belief in these arguments is demonstrated by its eager expansion of practical military cooperation with America in Asia and its increasing building of ADF capabilities designed to join US operations against China. The announcement last September of the AUKUS arrangements to acquire nuclear submarine technology, among other forms of cooperation, was another big step down this path. It now seems likely that US combat forces will soon be permanently based here. That could quite possibly extend to intermediate-range ballistic missiles aimed at China, perhaps with nuclear warheads. It is also likely that Canberra will soon agree to permanently deploy forces such as warships and combat aircraft to US bases in the region to be closer to the fight if war comes. All this suggests that Australia's choice has already been made.

But it is not that simple. Our alliance credentials in Washington will count for little if America ceases to play a substantial role in Asia, because we are a valuable ally only as long as America has a strong position in East Asia to sustain. It is important to be clear about this. Australia's alliance with America is said to spring from shared values and ideals, but history suggests otherwise. The only robust foundation for any serious alliance – one that imposes significant costs on its parties – is a clear alignment of interests and objectives. US and Australian interests have aligned since 1951 because America has sought to preserve strategic primacy in East Asia, and an alliance with Australia has helped it to do that. If America, under pressure from China, abandons that objective and ceases to seek any substantial strategic role in the region, then it will have no need for an alliance with Australia. Whatever Australians might hope, it is unrealistic to expect that American commitment to a substantial alliance would endure once the US objectives it was created to serve had been abandoned. Australia would find itself alone in Asia, without an expectation of great-power support, for the first time since European settlement.

And whether or not America chooses to fight, a crisis over Taiwan would most likely see its position destroyed. This is the real flaw in America's position, and Australia's. Washington cannot preserve its leadership in Asia whatever it does in response to a Chinese move against Taiwan. If it steps back from a fight, its credibility with allies, friends and rivals alike would be shattered. But its credibility would be equally shattered if it plunges into a war it cannot win. That means Australia has nothing to gain and much to lose by encouraging America to go to war over Taiwan, because no contribution we could offer would make US victory more likely, and nothing we could do would sustain our alliance with an America which, whether it chose peace or war, had destroyed its strategic position in Asia and therefore its need for an alliance with Australia.

This, then, is the true significance of the Taiwan issue for Australia. If America cannot defend Taiwan, it cannot sustain the position in Asia on which Australia has depended so completely for so long. It might once have been possible for Washington to negotiate some kind of accommodation with Beijing to preserve a significant, if reduced, regional role, but that chance has now almost certainly passed. This means that quite soon – probably within a decade – America's era as a major strategic player in East Asia will have passed, just as the much longer era of major European influence passed many years ago. The affairs of Asia will then be shaped by Asian powers, not outsiders, and those who rely on outsiders to secure their place in the regional order will be disappointed. Taiwan must work out its future relationship with Beijing as best it can, and so must Australia. That is our destiny in the Asian Century.

It will be a hard business, with no scope for sentimentality, wishful thinking or political grandstanding – nor for making promises we cannot keep. America's promise to defend Taiwan is no longer strategically or militarily credible, and maintaining it does more harm than good. It encourages the Taiwanese to expect that America can save them from Chinese aggression. And it imposes pressures on Washington to plunge into a war it cannot win, and which would inflict immense costs on itself and the whole of Asia. Australia, recognising this, should make it clear to Washington and to Taipei, publicly and privately, that it does not support such promises, and it would not join America in a war over Taiwan. ■

UNFINISHED BUSINESS

Xi's obsession with Taiwan

Linda Jakobson

On 22 May 1995, the Clinton administration announced that President Lee Teng-hui had been granted a visa to give a speech at his alma mater, Cornell University. Beijing was furious. Lee would be the first president from the Republic of China (ROC) – Taiwan's official name – to set foot on American soil since Washington broke off diplomatic ties with Taipei in 1979 and recognised Beijing as the sole legitimate representative of China. I remember listening to the news in Beijing and wondering what the government of the People's Republic of China (PRC) would do, besides merely denouncing the decision, to display its anger. From Beijing's viewpoint, its "one China" principle was being undermined and if this trend continued, American and regional support for an independent Taiwan would gather momentum.

Beijing's response came forty-six days later. Xinhua news agency announced that the People's Liberation Army (PLA) would conduct missile tests in the waters near Taiwan from 21 to 28 July. Those first tests were followed by more tests, as well as live ammunition exercises and joint PLA naval and air force exercises including highly publicised amphibious assault exercises. Beijing wanted to make it absolutely clear to Washington that the US commitment to a one China policy meant that senior Taiwanese officials were not permitted to visit the United States. Taiwan was not to be allowed space on the international stage.

Tensions between Beijing and Washington soared, especially after US aircraft carrier *Nimitz* and four escort vessels passed through the Taiwan Strait in December. Three months later, on the eve of the first democratic presidential elections in Taiwan, President Bill Clinton dispatched two aircraft carrier battle groups to the region, sparking fears that the PRC and the United States were on the brink of war.

Fast-forward twenty-six years and one cannot avoid a sense of déjà vu.

The repeated sorties by PLA aircraft into Taiwan's Air Defence Identification Zone (although keeping within international airspace) have served many functions, including trying to intimidate Taiwan and display the PLA's growing military might. Above all, as in 1995–96, the PLA's actions today reflect Beijing's anger and determination to signal that a formal separation between the mainland and Taiwan is unacceptable.

Since taking office a year ago, US president Joe Biden has continued the Trump administration's policies aimed at normalising Taiwan's international engagement. Now other countries are following suit. In 1995, PRC officials said to me privately: "If we don't stop this kind of movement towards a separate Taiwan, we will wake up one day to the US demand that we accept Taiwanese independence." There is no doubt that the same is being said in Beijing today.

After the 1995–96 Taiwan Strait Crisis, analysts such as Robert Ross delved into the details of the ten-month period of elevated tensions: the governments in Beijing, Taipei and Washington engaged in many types of signalling, to each other and to domestic audiences, and negotiated quietly behind closed doors. Ross concluded that none of the three parties had any intention to go to war. "China used coercive diplomacy to threaten costs until the United States and Taiwan changed their policies," Ross writes in his 2009 book. "The United States used deterrence diplomacy to communicate both to the Chinese and regional leaders the credibility of its strategic commitments."

Xi's patience is wearing thin

Now, as in 1995–96, no one wants war. Beijing continues to rely on coercive diplomacy and Washington on deterrence diplomacy. However, it would be a mistake to presume that the current fraught cross-Strait situation will be defused as it has been so many times over the past seven decades. Tensions have waxed and waned ever since Chiang Kai-shek and his defeated Nationalist (Kuomintang) troops fled to Taiwan in 1949 after the post–World War II Chinese Civil War and the capital of the Republic of China moved from Nanjing on the mainland to Taipei, Taiwan's largest city.

Today's tensions are more precarious than ever because all three parties instrumental to Taiwan's future – Taiwan, the PRC and the United States – have changed their approach.

What hasn't changed is the unbending persistence by the PRC that Taiwan is part of China. And that the PLA will use force if necessary to deter Taiwanese independence.

Whether peace can be maintained across the Strait will depend on above all, which path PRC president Xi Jinping takes to achieve unification, which, in his words, is "an inevitable requirement for the great rejuvenation of the Chinese people".

Cross-Strait tensions

Taiwan is becoming more and more repulsed by the authoritarian policies of Xi and less and less inclined to consider a future linked together with the PRC. The United States under Biden has continued the Trump administration's policy of treating Taiwan as a normal country in new subtle ways, while asserting it still upholds Washington's commitment to officially recognise only "one China" – the one that the PRC represents. And in Beijing, Xi's patience is wearing thin. Importantly, the PRC government has become increasingly vexed with actions in support of Taiwan by the United States and others. Beijing is desperate to stop what it sees as creeping efforts that will lead to recognition by the international community of a separate, independent Taiwan.

Several additional factors have changed over the past years. These are severely straining the peace that has prevailed for more than five decades.

First, Xi has explicitly said he is no longer content to patiently wait for unification to materialise "one day" and wants to oversee unification in his lifetime. Before Xi, the Communist Party of China (CPC) grudgingly tolerated the status quo and put unification to one side while trying to win the hearts and minds of the Taiwanese people through lucrative trade, investment and business opportunities. But Xi's exact words in 2019 were that unification "should not be left to future generations". This is a direct rebuttal of Deng Xiaoping's pragmatic approach to the Taiwan dilemma. Deng's tacit acceptance of kicking the can down the road laid the foundation of peace despite repeated pledges by every CPC leader since Deng that unification is paramount.

Second, the PRC has become more assertive in the past few years, alarming policymakers in Washington and across the region. Xi has proven less risk-averse than his predecessors.

Third, the PLA's modernisation drive undertaken over the last twenty-plus years has shifted the balance of military power in the Taiwan Strait unequivocally to the PRC. Six years ago, the US Office of Naval Intelligence already assessed that the PRC has a technologically advanced and flexible force that (without US intervention) gives Beijing the capability to conduct a military campaign successfully within the first island chain (for instance, to take Taiwan or the Senkaku Islands).

In particular, the PRC has enhanced its anti-access/area denial (A2/AD) capabilities, which are designed to deny freedom of movement to potential adversaries, especially the United States, and prevent them from intervening in a conflict near the PRC's coast or from attacking the Chinese mainland. If hostilities erupted, it would be unthinkable for US aircraft carrier *Nimitz* to breeze through the Taiwan Strait, as it did in 1995.

Fourth, relations between Beijing and Washington have deteriorated markedly in the past few years. The political mood in Washington is strikingly anti-China. In a city where Republicans and Democrats are at loggerheads, the one issue they agree on is that the United States must curb Xi's ambitions. Xi, in turn, has stirred up domestic nationalists by emphasising the need to "put all our minds and energies in preparing for war and remain on high alert".

Fifth, the economic interdependence and people-to-people engagement between the PRC and Taiwan continues to deepen despite political tensions. What is often lost in analysis is that Taiwan's prosperity is heavily dependent on the PRC, and that hundreds of thousands of Taiwanese live permanently in the PRC. Taiwan is extremely reliant on exports to the PRC despite efforts to diversify. In 2020, close to 44 per cent of Taiwan's exports went to the PRC (including Hong Kong), a 14 per cent increase from 2019. The value of exports was equivalent to about 15 per cent of Taiwan's GDP in 2020. For comparison, Australia's exports to the PRC in 2020 were equivalent to 8 per cent of its GDP.

What has further changed in the last decade is the composition of those exports and the PRC's increasing reliance on sophisticated

Taiwanese integrated circuits (ICs), which are used in semiconductor chips and the manufacture of several advanced technologies such as aerospace components and electric vehicles. Every other Taiwanese industry continues to be of secondary importance in PRC–Taiwan trade, despite the Trump administration's restrictions on selling ICs with American components to the PRC. The PRC is a major exporter of less advanced ICs but needs to import the more sophisticated versions.

The PRC is making concerted efforts to decrease its dependence on imported semiconductors. How this dependence will impact the cross-Strait dynamic is unclear. The PRC wants access to Taiwanese semiconductor technology; on the other hand, a military conflict would disrupt and possibly devastate Taiwan's high-tech manufacturing capabilities.

Beijing regards Taiwan as a renegade province and treats it as such

Hong Kong turned the tide

Taiwan, the PRC and the United States are all constantly trying to change the status quo. This complex situation is further complicated by the fact that all three parties interpret the status quo differently.

From Taiwan's viewpoint, the status quo means that the island functions independently and is a self-governed democracy. Taiwan has its own currency and military. Taiwanese use passports that say

"Republic of China" (the country established in 1911 by the Nationalists) and fly the ROC flag. Self-rule in Taiwan's case means de facto rather than de jure independence.

In Taiwan, negative attitudes toward unification have increased since Xi Jinping rose to power in 2012, and have become even stronger since Beijing's crackdown on civil liberties in Hong Kong. Taiwanese voted in Tsai Ing-wen, Taiwan's president, for a second term to a large extent because of her unambiguous support for the Hong Kong demonstrators and pledge that Taiwan would not become the next Hong Kong: "As long as I'm president, one country, two systems will never be an option." An overwhelming number of Taiwanese – 82.8 per cent, according to 2021 polling – reject the PRC's "one country two systems" model for unification. Even before Xi, a sense of separate national identity among Taiwanese was growing. Today, polls show that 63.3 per cent of Taiwanese identify solely as Taiwanese, not Chinese.

From Washington's perspective, the key facet of the status quo is conflict avoidance. The Biden administration brushes off Beijing's accusations that its current actions contradict its commitment recognising the government of the PRC as the sole legal government of China. This commitment, which acknowledges the PRC position that Taiwan is part of China, was made in 1979 when Washington switched diplomatic recognition from Taipei to Beijing. The commitment also acknowledges that the United States has the right to maintain cultural, commercial and other unofficial relations with the people of Taiwan.

Taiwan is a bleeding ulcer

From the viewpoint of the CPC, the unresolved political status of Taiwan is a bleeding ulcer. It is a reminder that the Chinese Civil War remains unfinished, that the CPC has not yet fulfilled its mission to "reunify" China. Xi Jinping has clearly stated that "resolving the Taiwan question is ... the unshakeable commitment of the Communist Party of China. It is also a shared aspiration of all the sons and daughters of the Chinese nation."

As so often happens in long-standing territorial disputes, the parties do not even agree on terminology. While both sides use the same word in Chinese – *tongyi* – in English, the PRC uses the term "reunification" and Taiwan uses "unification", as it has never been part of Communist China. After Japan's defeat in 1945, the ROC assumed the administration of the province of Taiwan, which had been a Japanese colony since 1895. The PRC, in turn, emphasises that before becoming a Japanese colony, Taiwan was part of Qing Dynasty China from 1683 to 1895.

The notion that Taiwan and mainland China will one day be unified is embedded in the CPC's public education. Taiwanese independence is a non-starter even for those PRC citizens who are critical of the Communist Party; even for those who feel Xi has unnecessarily provoked the United States; even for those who have visited Taiwan and admire its civil liberties and democratic politics. Meanwhile, on the other side of the Strait, public education in Taiwan since 2000 has emphasised a separate Taiwanese identity, to the degree that one might mistakenly think that Taiwanese culture is totally separate from

Chinese culture. More than 95 per cent of people in Taiwan and 92 per cent of the entire PRC population are of the same Han ethnic ancestry. On even a casual visit to Fujian province on the mainland, across the Strait from Taiwan, one is vividly reminded that Taiwanese and Fujianese worship the same gods at similar-looking temples, eat the same traditional foods, and have the same ancestor-worshipping traditions. At home and among friends, the majority of Fujianese and Taiwanese speak the same minnan dialect, while Mandarin is the official language on both sides. What separates them is their political systems. Fujianese live under one-party Communist rule; for over two decades, Taiwanese have lived in a vibrant democracy.

Beijing regards Taiwan as a renegade province and treats it as such. The PRC government refuses to address the Taiwanese president as "president", explicitly rejecting the legitimacy of Taiwanese elected officials, and instead uses "leader". Regardless of how strong and prosperous the PRC becomes, its leadership will not accept Taiwan's separateness. The pursuit of unification is central to CPC legitimacy.

All nations (except thirteen small ones and the Holy See) recognise Beijing as the sole representative of "one China". Beijing is resolute that Taiwan is not represented in any international body in which membership requires recognised nationhood, including the United Nations and its sub-organisations.

PRC officials take extreme actions to enforce Taiwan's international isolation. For example, in Perth in 2017, PRC participants caused a commotion by shouting and speaking into the microphone over the meeting's chairperson to protest the presence of Taiwanese delegates at the opening session of a Kimberley Process meeting to promote oversight of the diamond industry. The PRC participants would not relent until the Taiwanese delegation was ejected from the meeting. Even following natural disasters such as the Kobe earthquake, and during the Covid-19 pandemic, the PRC has insisted that international aid and communication about health measures must be conducted via Beijing.

Trump's intervention

For decades, Taiwan has aspired to break out of this international isolation, especially since transitioning to democracy in the 1990s. But until a few years ago, other nations heeded Beijing's demands that Taiwan cannot be treated

Even Canberra's previously timid attitude has changed

as a sovereign nation. Elaborate diplomatic language made it possible for Taiwan, the world's twentieth-largest economy by purchasing power parity, to join economic organisations, such as the Asia-Pacific Economic Cooperation (as "Chinese Taipei") and the World Trade Organization (as a "separate customs territory").

But, other than on issues directly related to Taiwan's economy, the rest of the world has avoided challenging Beijing. That is, until the Trump administration initiated low-key projects and policies intended to normalise Taiwan's international engagement. Washington allowed more high-level political interaction between Taipei and Washington; made public its official interaction; and found ingenious ways of circumventing Beijing's insistence on Taiwan's exclusion from any organisation requiring sovereignty.

The 2018 *Taiwan Travel Act* allows senior-level US officials to visit Taiwan and vice versa. In May 2019, US and Taiwanese national security chiefs met in Washington for the first time in more than forty years. In July 2019, Taiwan's President Tsai Ing-wen visited New York and Colorado while officially in transit to the Caribbean. She met with a state governor, UN ambassadors from Taiwan's diplomatic allies and members of the US Congress. These meetings were unprecedented. Another first was joint Taiwan–United States cyber exercises in 2019. They were aimed at foreign actors without singling out the PRC but were clearly a response to PRC cyberattacks. In August 2020, the Secretary of Health and Human Services became the highest-ranking US official to visit the island since 1979.

Biden has not veered far from Trump's policies. New guidelines encourage US officials to meet their Taiwanese counterparts. Biden has not ended the deployment of US special forces to conduct training in Taiwan. He blessed an agreement for US and Taiwanese coastguards to increase cooperation. He invited Taipei's top representative in the United States to his inauguration and allowed the US ambassador to Palau to visit Taiwan with the president of the Pacific country, both unprecedented moves. Biden, too, approved a robust arms package for Taiwan in August 2021.

The United States dropped all pretenses about its intentions regarding Taiwan when a US defense official said in December that Taiwan is strategically "critical to ... the defense of vital US interests in the Indo-Pacific". This Senate testimony by Assistant Defence Secretary Ely Ratner is the first public statement by a serving US official that makes clear what PRC officials in private have said for decades: that despite repeated assurances to the contrary the United States opposes unification, even if it takes place without coercion.

Beijing sternly rebuked each of these actions and statements. But the Biden administration has not shied away from backing Taiwan and openly drawing allies' and partners' attention to Taiwan's isolation and predicament.

Japan, too, has implemented more practical cooperation with Taiwan. Informally, there have been close ties between the two for years, both at the societal level and between their militaries. Although remarks by Japan's Minister of Defence Nonuo Kishi that "the peace and stability of Taiwan are directly connected to Japan" do not indicate a fundamental change in policy, as some media reports stated, they do reflect a shift in the Japanese government's willingness to publicly express support for Taiwan.

Even Canberra's previously timid attitude has changed. Australia has joined the chorus of voices expressing support for strengthening ties with Taiwan, a "critical partner" and a "leading democracy". Prime Minister Scott Morrison, previously careful to refer to Taiwan as an "economy" or a "jurisdiction", has referred to Taiwan as a "country" many times since May 2021 and emphasised that it is "a country that has done extraordinarily well". Considering the tense relations between Canberra and Beijing, the Australian government appears to have concluded that it does not have much to lose by following Washington's lead on Taiwan.

All of this increases Beijing's anxiety that the United States, Japan, Australia and others are eroding its adamant stance that Taiwan is not a country.

What will Xi do next?

How will Xi go about ensuring that "the historical task of the complete reunification of the motherland ... will definitely be fulfilled"?

The answer requires a word of caution. However unlikely it seems now, the possibility of the governments in Beijing and Taipei striking a deal to resolve Taiwan's political status cannot be ruled out. Few foresaw the demise of the Soviet Union. Anyone would have laughed in 1988 at the thought of Ukraine's future foreign policy challenges. The myriad of problems facing the PRC, coupled with an increasing disdain among PRC middle classes and elites for Xi's authoritarian measures, means one cannot completely dismiss the possibility of upheaval within the CPC, or even in the PRC itself.

If Taiwan's economy were to drastically falter, for whatever reason, and be on the brink of collapse, a Taiwanese leader could conceivably negotiate a symbolic but unified "Greater Chinese Union". It would be even more likely if Washington were to withdraw its support for

Taiwan, or if Taiwan's leaders seriously questioned the United States' reliability – as some observers post-Afghanistan have opined that they should – and deemed that Washington was not prepared to suffer body bags in a war over Taiwan.

One possible unification model would be for each entity to retain its system of government – in essence, functioning separately as they do today – and secure international safeguards for the demilitarisation of Taiwan. The leaders within this "Greater Chinese Union" would convene an annual meeting, rich with symbolism, to cherish Chinese civilisation. Ultimately, the so-called Taiwan problem is about the symbolism of sovereignty. Taiwan would be allowed to participate in the UN General Assembly and its sub-organisations via its own representative as part of a "Greater Chinese Union" delegation. The

The campaign could start ominously but relatively innocuously

PRC would achieve a reunification of sorts and Taiwan would break out of its international isolation. This solution – which I spelt out with Gareth Evans in a 2004 report for the International Crisis Group – is utopian in today's cross-Strait climate. It would, of course, dramatically transform the region's geopolitics.

Now to the question of how Xi could ensure that he becomes the PRC leader credited with unifying the mainland and Taiwan. Despite the recent barrage of statements by elected leaders, for example Peter

Dutton, warning of imminent war, a catastrophic military conflict is not the route Xi is most likely to choose. Just as Xi's warnings that the PLA will use force if necessary to deter Taiwan's independence are credible, so are his statements that unification by peaceful means is his preference. In a clear message to the alarmists, Xi used unprecedented language to underline the preferred avenue to unification in his virtual meeting with Joe Biden in November: "We have patience and will strive for the prospect of peaceful reunification with utmost sincerity and efforts."

The costs and risks to the PRC of any full-scale war in the Taiwan Strait would be enormous. Anything short of complete victory and unification would be disastrous for the CPC. War is not in Xi's interest.

Military conflict cannot be ruled out. A crisis arising from an accidental clash between aircraft or vessels could spiral out of control but is unlikely.

A more likely scenario is a protracted and intensive PRC campaign using "all means short of war" to force the Taiwanese leadership to start negotiating premised on the precondition that it acknowledges that there is only "one China". Taiwan has hitherto insisted that it is willing to hold political talks with Beijing but only as an equal without preconditions. However, Taiwan has de facto stipulated its own preconditions, namely that the PRC abandon its threat of force and accept that the future of Taiwan must be decided by its 23 million people.

'Measures short of war' is a term traditionally used to describe all ways and means available to achieve strategic objectives without crossing the line into major conventional (or nuclear) confrontation. In other words, violence is used as a tool to shift popular support to achieve political ends rather than as a tool to defeat another country's military forces.

In an attempt to break Taiwan's will, Beijing could adopt an aggressive mix of new technologies and conventional methods. These range from intimidation via economic pressure or a partial embargo, cyberattacks, disinformation operations and covert actions of political interference and subversion, to assassination and the limited use of military force. Once political talks have started, Xi could declare success for having paved the way to unification. Talks could take years, but Xi would be lauded for bringing the nation closer to complete unification, a central tenet of the "China Dream".

How to break Taiwan's will without all-out war

In this scenario, the PRC would not invade Taiwan. Rather, Beijing would strive to create utter chaos in Taiwan and compel the government in Taipei to accept the one China principle and negotiate a future unification model. In the beginning, it would be impossible to pinpoint who was behind the destabilising actions. Few shots would be fired other than for possible political assassinations. Taiwan's armed forces would struggle to counter Beijing's actions. The United States and others would find it difficult to assist Taiwan other than by strongly condemning Beijing.

No single action by the PRC would warrant a military response by Taiwan or the United States. The campaign could start ominously but relatively innocuously. For example, mainland Chinese officials would gather major Taiwanese investors in the PRC (known for their support of maintaining friendly ties to Beijing) and insist that they sign a letter calling on Taiwan's president to open cross-Strait political talks. Refusal to sign would result in business difficulties, the investors would be told. The Beijing government would at the same time send a letter to the Taiwanese "leader" calling for immediate consultations to address political differences and establish ways to work together towards reunification. On the same day, Beijing could suddenly cut Taiwan's air routes to PRC cities drastically, stating that foreign airlines needed those routes. International airlines would be told to choose between flying to the PRC or Taiwan. PRC combat aircraft would go further than on current missions and violate Taiwanese air space.

Taiwan's stock market could be expected to plunge. PRC-backed media outlets would run scare campaigns. Some groups would demand a formal declaration of independence; others would demand that the government open talks with Beijing. Protesters would take to the streets. Confrontations between opposing political groups could become violent, and police would be forced to use tear gas to disperse crowds. Gangs could attack independence supporters.

In this scenario, the PRC would next launch a barrage of sophisticated cyber-attacks with the aim of first disrupting, then shutting down electricity and telecommunications on the island. At the same time, the PLA would initiate extensive military exercises. A flotilla of PLA Navy ships would sail close to Taiwan's coast. During the live-fire portion of missile exercises near Taiwan, one of the missiles would "stray" off course and cause civilian casualties in Taiwan. Meanwhile, tens of thousands of unarmed PRC fishermen would make their way across the Strait on a "Mission of Friendship to Promote Reunification", trusting that Taiwan's armed forces would not open fire and slaughter unarmed people en masse. Some of the fishermen – many of them paramilitary in disguise – would be "invited" ashore by Taiwanese who support Beijing. Cut-off from communications, rumours of the PRC's intentions would run wild though Taiwan's darkened cities. The PLA Navy would start operations to impose a partial blockade of the four harbours on the west coast of Taiwan. Beijing would demand other governments shut their representative offices in Taipei. At the end of a period of intensive pressure, the

By dismissing the eternal status quo, Xi has taken a big gamble

People's Daily would publish an editorial encouraging Chinese brethren in Taiwan to carefully assess their interests and make the right decision, warning that the clock is ticking.

The determination of Hong Kong residents in the face of formidable pressure stands as a reminder that human willpower should not be underestimated. However, it is impossible to predict how resilient the Taiwanese people under siege would be. There are simply too many unknown variables: What would be the role of Taiwanese who favour unification in this scenario? What proportion of pro-unification Taiwanese would act as proxies for the PRC? Of the population,

1.9 per cent (which translates into 444,000 Taiwanese) want unification as soon as possible, according to a September 2021 survey by Taiwan's Mainland Affairs Council. Approximately 5 per cent (1.2 million people) favour the status quo for now and want unification later. Although these pro-unification individuals represent a small minority, their actions could be decisive.

How many Taiwanese would, amid an intense and frightening crisis, prefer that their government negotiate a compromise to avoid an escalation of violence? After all, in this scenario, the Beijing government would time and again remind Taiwanese that all it is asking for is a commitment from Taiwan's leaders to negotiate.

When will Xi make a move?

When could Xi launch an exhaustive pressure campaign using "all means short of war"?

The state of the PRC economy will be a decisive factor, as will the state of PRC–United States relations and Xi's own political standing. Some observers predict that the dissatisfaction across PRC society stemming from serious energy shortages will prompt Xi to use a Taiwan crisis in the near future to divert attention. That is unlikely.

It is more likely that the next inflection point will be Taiwan's presidential election in 2024. Political pressure on Xi to make progress toward his stated goal of "reunification" will intensify after that. He has backed himself into a corner and could feel compelled to act decisively if the next Taiwanese president is an openly pro-independence leader who, contrary to Tsai, intentionally stirs up nationalist emotions among Taiwanese. It is hard to imagine the seven members of the CPC Politburo – the PRC's most powerful political body – convincing themselves that time is still on their side if a steadfast independence proponent such as Tsai's current vice-president, William Lai, is elected. CPC leaders cannot indefinitely ignore the trend that as older generation mainland-born Taiwanese die, the proportion of Taiwanese who feel strongly about their separate identity and democracy grows.

Before the twenty-first Party Congress in late 2027, Xi could decide that he needs to display strength to maintain his grip on power. That is also the year that the CPC has decreed the PLA should be a fully modern military. The PLA needs to be ready if a concerted pressure campaign using all "means short of war" suddenly turns into a military conflict. This is entirely possible.

A key question for which there is no definitive answer is whether Xi Jinping has put unification above other national priorities. Thus far he has not, and he continues to send mixed signals about his intentions, such as his remarks about peaceful unification to Joe Biden in November.

By dismissing the eternal status quo, Xi has taken a big gamble. If war breaks out across the Taiwan Strait, the ensuing devastation will stymie economic development and crush people's hopes for a more prosperous tomorrow in the PRC. That, too, is central to Xi's legacy and CPC legitimacy. Xi might well regret not taking Deng Xiaoping's advice: "Achieving national unification is the nation's wish, if not unified in 100 years, then unified in 1000 years." ■

THE EQUATION

What would a Taiwan war look like?

Brendan Taylor

A full-blown conflict over Taiwan could make living through the COVID-19 pandemic seem like a cakewalk. It would very likely be the most devastating war in history, drawing the world's major powers into their first nuclear exchange. Hundreds of millions could perish, both from the fighting itself and from the sickening after-effects of radiation. Even a limited nuclear conflict would be an environmental nightmare, with soot from incinerated cities shutting out the sun's rays, depleting food supplies and plunging the planet into a prolonged famine. Life for Australians would be forever changed. Such a catastrophe looms closer than we think. If it eventuates, those left behind after Asia's atomic mushroom clouds have settled will wish that we had fought with every fibre of our being to prevent it.

As China's wealth and power have grown, so too have its military options for conquering Taiwan. Indeed, the lack of such options prompted Beijing's massive military modernisation, which began right after the Taiwan Strait crisis of 1995–96. During that crisis, the United States forced Beijing to back down by dispatching two aircraft carrier battle groups to waters close to Taiwan. This was, at the time, the largest US naval deployment to Asia since the Vietnam War. China's leaders vowed to never again suffer such humiliation.

China now has a range of ways to attack Taiwan. The quickest and dirtiest option is a missile strike, using the 2000-plus short- and medium-range missiles currently trained on the island. Alternatively, China could try strangling Taiwan's 23 million people into submission by blockading food and fuel supplies. The island imports 80–90 per cent of its food and close to 100 per cent of its oil. Either option could be complemented by industrial-scale cyberwarfare, plunging one of the most interconnected societies on Earth into darkness and causing widespread panic and confusion.

The most ambitious and challenging military option is a full-scale amphibious assault. An estimated 1 to 2 million People's Liberation Army (PLA) troops would need to be ferried across the Taiwan Strait in a massive armada of military and civilian ships. This turbulent body of water – 128 kilometres at its narrowest point and 410 kilometres at its widest – is notorious for its strong currents, dense fog and inclement weather. This means that such an invasion would most likely occur either between late March and the end of April, or from late September to the end of October, when the waters are at their calmest. Moreover, the natural obstacles confronting China's invading force are not only maritime. Taiwan's rugged east coast consists of steep cliffs that shoot straight out of the sea, while its western flank is lined with dense mud-flats that are not conducive to troop landings. Nonetheless, as the mainland's amphibious lift capabilities continue to expand, China's option to invade becomes increasingly viable.

However, because this would be the largest and riskiest amphibious landing operation in history, many commentators maintain that China's strongman leader, Xi Jinping, will most likely take a graduated approach to conflict. He might start with a missile strike or cyberattack, for instance, testing and hoping to bend the will of the Taiwanese people. Should that fail, Xi could tighten the screws with a blockade. If Taiwanese resistance continued, Xi might then – and only then – issue the order to invade.

This interpretation aligns with the ancient Chinese strategy of "winning without fighting". Most recently, Beijing has successfully employed this approach in the South China Sea, using a mix of so-called "grey zone" tactics – such as deploying large fishing fleets known as "maritime militia" to occupy disputed areas – that are short of military force but which chip away at the status quo to create new facts on the ground. Applying this template limits the risk of Beijing's worst nightmare: US military intervention in support of Taiwan. Would Washington risk nuclear war and the possible loss of major American cities in response to a Chinese cyberattack against the island? Would US president Joe Biden *really* order the US Navy to fire upon a defence-less swarm of Chinese fishing vessels supporting a blockade?

Escalation and miscalculation

This conventional wisdom that China will likely attack Taiwan incrementally recalls Herman Kahn's famous "escalation ladder". Kahn, an eccentric American Cold War strategist who is rumoured to have inspired Stanley Kubrick's satirical character Dr Strangelove, believed that all types of conflict – even nuclear – could ultimately be managed and controlled. His 44-rung escalation ladder sought to model the steps that leaders might take in a real-world crisis. It tried to capture the growing dangers of antagonists ascending higher and the crisis deepening, along with the choices available at each step to climb down and avert Armageddon.

In a Taiwan conflict, escalation will be neither linear nor predictable

But times and technologies have changed since the height of the Cold War. In a Taiwan conflict, escalation will be neither linear nor predictable. Many of the traditional distinctions, or so-called "firebreaks", between conventional and nuclear weapons are increasingly blurred. During the Cold War, for instance, the systems that the United States used to warn of a Soviet nuclear strike were located separately, either in space or at remote geographic locations, making them difficult to target. Today, they are integrated with conventional situational awareness and strategic warning systems. Likewise, many of Beijing's newer missiles – such as the Dongfeng 26 (DF-26) ballistic missile, known as the "carrier killer" for its capacity to target US aircraft carriers up to 4000 kilometres away – are "dual use", meaning they can carry either a conventional or a nuclear payload.

Inspired by a combination of theoretical physics and science fiction, the American analyst Rebecca Hersman recently observed that Kahn's escalation ladder has been usurped by what she terms "wormhole escalation". Wormholes, as physicists including Albert Einstein have long theorised, are bridges or shortcuts between two different points in space-time. Hersman has applied this concept to conflict situations to illustrate how contemporary crises can escalate far more rapidly and unpredictably than Kahn's well-worn metaphor anticipates. As she explained, such crises are risky and precarious – they do not progress "stepwise" because they have no "clear thresholds between behavior that would elicit a conventional or nuclear response".

Given the unimaginable consequences, a nuclear conflict over Taiwan is far more likely to be the product of accident rather than design. It could be triggered by something as simple as an unintended collision of Chinese and Taiwanese fighters flying over the Taiwan Strait, or by a stand-off between US and Chinese ships operating in the waters below, where an exchange of fire results in one of the vessels foundering. From there, events could easily spiral out of control.

This is hardly the stuff of fiction. Chinese incursions into the waters and skies around Taiwan have ramped up substantially in recent years. Over four days in early October 2021, during China's National Day celebrations, Beijing sent a record 149 aircraft into Taiwan's so-called Air Defence Identification Zone (ADIZ), including its nuclear-capable H-6 bombers. Unlike in the past, where Taiwanese fighter aircraft typically monitored such encroachments from a distance, the island's president, Tsai Ing-wen, has pledged to "forcibly expel" them if they transgress the Taiwan Strait's median line, the unofficial maritime boundary that separated China and Taiwan for two decades before Beijing summarily dismissed its existence in September 2020. During that same month, Taiwan's air force reportedly outmanoeuvred and drove a Chinese fighter out of the island's ADIZ.

Such a crisis could also be sparked by human error. On 1 July 2016, for instance, a Taiwanese navy vessel accidentally fired an anti-shipping missile in China's direction. The missile flew for approximately 120 kilometres before striking a Taiwanese fishing boat near Taiwan's Penghu Islands,

Defeat in a Taiwan conflict would provoke domestic backlash, challenging Xi's authority and possibly even the legitimacy of the CCP

killing its captain and injuring three of its crew. But what if such an incident had occurred five years later, in the nationalistically charged atmosphere of the Chinese Communist Party's centenary celebrations? And what if the missile had hit a Chinese fishing boat, a PLA Navy vessel or, worse still, reached the mainland? Could the resultant crisis have been contained?

Cooler heads might have still prevailed. Yet in any future crisis over Taiwan where the US military becomes involved, the risks of "wormhole escalation" cannot be underestimated. As soon as the shooting starts, significant "first mover" advantages will be available to both sides. The reason is simple. Modern militaries rely on a sophisticated network of radars, sonars and satellites to track an opponent's movements. Such systems are vulnerable and difficult to defend. Taking them out is tremendously provocative, but confers decisive advantages by essentially blinding an opponent.

The temptation to pull off such a risky military manoeuvre may ultimately prove irresistible for Xi in the heat of conflict. Despite the considerable benefits conferred by geography – the island of Taiwan is 11,000 kilometres away from the continental United States – China remains well behind America in some key areas of militarily capability. A June 2021 report from the highly respected International Institute for Strategic Studies (IISS), for instance, estimates that China's cyber capabilities – regarded by some analysts as the sine qua non of modern warfare – are at least a decade behind those of the US.

Likewise, China's nuclear capabilities remain minuscule compared to America's. China has 350 nuclear warheads; America has 3800. China also has only six submarines – the so-called Type 094 Jin-class nuclear-powered, ballistic missile-carrying submarine (SSBN) – that can deliver a nuclear strike. Such asymmetries mean that Beijing lacks what is called a secure "second strike" capability – the means to hit back at an opponent even after they have unleashed a devastating nuclear attack.

Xi is working assiduously to address this imbalance. In mid-2021, three freshly built fields of nuclear launch silos were discovered in north-central China by US-based analysts using commercial satellite imagery. The Pentagon estimates that China's nuclear arsenal will swell to 1000 warheads by 2030. Construction of China's next-generation SSBN (the Type 96 class) is also underway, along with a new kind of long-range, submarine-launched ballistic missile known as the JL-3. But such developments take time, as shown by Australia's difficulties in deciding its next generation of submarine. Until these advancements come online, China's nuclear vulnerabilities will encourage Beijing to embrace a "use them or lose them" mentality in a Taiwan conflict, reinforcing the risks of wormhole escalation.

A dangerous decade

China's great military leaps forward can't be underestimated. Modelling produced by the RAND Corporation, a leading American think tank, suggests that US forces would have made easy work of their Chinese counterparts in the 1995–96 Taiwan Strait crisis. RAND estimates that it would have taken only a single air wing of US fighters (or seventy-two aircraft) around a week to establish air superiority over the Taiwan Strait. At that time, China's land forces were the largest in the world but its air and naval capabilities were antiquated and weak. Beijing couldn't have even struck nearby US military bases on Okinawa.

Recent Pentagon wargaming exercises highlight how far China's military has come. These simulations routinely end in American defeat. Undoubtedly, such results should be taken with a grain of salt.

Wargames are generally designed to stretch participants, often unduly advantaging one's hypothetical opponent. That said, what was once considered inconceivable – China defeating the United States in a Taiwan conflict – is now a possibility.

Following its humiliating backdown in the mid-1990s, Beijing began building its so-called "anti-access area denial" (or A2/AD) capabilities. These are the tools that a country uses to prevent an opponent from operating freely within a particular geographic area, or from even entering that area. Successful A2/AD relies upon a "family" of weapons and systems, including powerful anti-shipping missiles; the platforms needed to deliver these – such as mobile land-based launchers, fast and stealthy surface ships, fighter and bomber aircraft, and submarines; as well as the satellites, sonars and radars required to locate and target the enemy. Taken together, the chief purpose of Beijing's burgeoning A2/AD capabilities is to force America to operate as far away from this flashpoint as possible, nullifying its influence in a cross-Strait conflict.

One school of thought claims that Beijing already believes it can present Taipei with a fait accompli before US military help arrives and that Xi, perceiving an historic opportunity, will move to take Taiwan sooner rather than later. According to this line of thinking, Xi sees a deeply divided America that has been badly wounded by the devastating social and economic impacts of the pandemic, and wearied by protracted military campaigns in the Middle East. He senses a depleted US military whose distracted masters have been caught flat-footed by both the pace and scale of China's challenge, to which they are only now beginning to react. In March 2021, US Indo-Pacific Commander Admiral Philip S. Davidson fuelled such speculation, suggesting during Congressional testimony that China could move to take Taiwan in the next six years.

This seems unlikely. Despite the impressive gains that China's military has made over the past quarter-century, Xi cannot yet be certain of its ability to take Taiwan by force. Failure is not an option. Another humiliating backdown or, worse still, defeat at the hands of the US military would strike at the heart of Xi's signature "Chinese Dream" – his plan to make China so wealthy and powerful that it is never again subjected to the ignominy suffered during the so-called "Century of Humiliation" (1839–1949), when the Middle Kingdom was carved up by a succession of foreign powers. Defeat in a Taiwan conflict would provoke domestic backlash, challenging Xi's authority and possibly even the legitimacy of the CCP. With that much at stake, Xi will not move capriciously.

Time is also on Xi's side. As both the quality and quantity of China's A2/AD capabilities increase, Beijing's ability to hold America at arm's length militarily will improve. China's navy is already larger than America's, while approximately 70 per cent of its fleet is considered modern by contemporary shipbuilding standards. America's main military bases on Okinawa and Guam are well within range of China's DF-26 missiles. Two leading American military experts, Ian Easton and Oriana Skylar Mastro, estimate that the US would lose at least 70 per cent of aircraft based at its front-line Kadena Air Base on Okinawa during the opening salvoes of a Taiwan conflict. Based on these trends, and barring any game-changing technological breakthroughs by the US military, a tipping point will be reached within the next decade where America largely loses the ability to come to Taiwan's defence.

Ironically, as panic sets in, conflict may not be triggered by Beijing, but by Taipei or Washington.

In Taiwan, memories of the Chinese Civil War (1927–49) – which created the current cross-Strait stand-off – are fading, especially among the younger generations, who have little affinity with the mainland, and a powerful sense of Taiwanese identity is emerging. When polling on such matters began in the early 1990s, almost half (46.4 per cent) of the island's inhabitants identified as "both Taiwanese and Chinese", 25.5 per cent as "Chinese" and 17.6 per cent as "Taiwanese". Today, 62.3 per cent regard themselves as "exclusively Taiwanese" and a mere 2.8 per cent as "Chinese". An even smaller 1.4 per cent of Taiwanese favour unification with the mainland. A July 2020 survey conducted by Taiwan's National Chengchi University found that almost half (48.7 per cent) of the population instead support a Taiwanese declaration of independence, even if this provokes a Chinese attack. Almost 70 per cent of voters from Tsai's Democratic Progressive Party (DPP) are of this view.

Tsai has skilfully navigated between rising pro-independence sentiment in her own ranks and increased Chinese bullying. Unlike Xi, however, she will not be Taiwan's leader for life. Taiwanese presidents serve a maximum of two four-year terms, and the Tsai era will end in 2024. After that, all bets are off. A leader resembling former DPP president Chen Shui-bian, whose pro-independence antics had to be reined in by Washington during the mid-2000s, could take the helm. Tsai's deputy, William Lai, a likely presidential candidate, once described himself as a "Taiwan independence worker". He has moderated this stance while working for Tsai, but it is conceivable he might revert, as leader, to his pro-independence roots.

As America loses its military grip on this flashpoint, there is also a risk that Washington will over-compensate and inadvertently spark a clash. The turbulent Trump presidency was heading in that direction. Trump approved a record US$18 billion worth of US arms

Taiwan's 23 million people could opt for a desperate declaration of independence

sales to Taiwan. American warships sailed monthly through the Taiwan Strait. Major policy documents, such as the US Defense Department's June 2019 *Indo-Pacific Strategy Report*, referred to Taiwan as a country for the first time. During the administration's dying days, as pro-Trump rioters stormed the Capitol, Secretary of State Mike Pompeo dropped a bombshell of his own by lifting longstanding restrictions on contact between US and Taiwanese officials.

Joe Biden shows little sign of reversing course. He too broke with tradition by inviting Taiwan's top envoy to the US, Hsiao Bi-khim, to his inauguration. Biden raised eyebrows again in August 2021, when, during a live television interview, he stated that America's "sacred" commitments to its NATO allies were analogous to those with Japan, South Korea and Taiwan. The White House immediately walked back this assertion, insisting that US policy on Taiwan had not changed. Yet an October 2021 CNN 'town hall' interview suggests otherwise. Asked twice by anchor Anderson Cooper whether the United States will come to Taiwan's defence if China attacks, Biden replied without hesitation: "Yes, we have a commitment to do that."

The coming decade will be a dangerous one. China's capacity to annex the island and, more importantly, to force America to operate further away will improve. As the power balance tilts in Beijing's favour, the pressures on Washington to consider a forceful resolution of its own, while it still credibly can, will also intensify.

Taiwan's dilemmas are gravest. The island's best hope is for political transformation on the mainland, where CCP rule collapses and is replaced by some form of democracy. But hope is not a strategy, particularly for such an improbable outcome. Unification under Chinese rule is also a non-starter. The Taiwanese have long been leery of China's "one country, two systems" formula for Hong Kong, which was supposed to afford that territory some autonomy after the British handover. Beijing's worsening repression there confirms Taiwan's worst fears. Faced with an impossible set of choices, Taiwan's 23 million people could opt for a desperate declaration of independence. Yet if Beijing responds militarily, they have the most to lose.

Diplomacy now

A Taiwan conflict, however it plays out, would be devastating. RAND estimates that during a year-long war, China's gross domestic product would drop by 25–35 per cent. Much of the western Pacific Ocean, including the 3.7 million square kilometres of the South China Sea, would be too dangerous for commercial shipping and aircraft. This is not the worst-case scenario. RAND's modelling assumes that any conflict over Taiwan will stay below the nuclear threshold because US and Chinese leaders wouldn't risk such an exchange. That assumption is too optimistic.

A Taiwan conflict would change life as Australians know it. The conflict's North-East Asian epicentre is home to three of this country's largest trading partners: China, Japan and South Korea. Australia could run out of fuel. In 2018, alarming media reports suggested Australia's oil stocks would only last twenty-two days in the event of a crisis, well below the ninety days required by international law. Efforts to redress this vulnerability came in April 2020, when the government splashed $94 million on a new "strategic fuel reserve". But these supplies are stored in the United States, and there is no guarantee of their reaching Australian shores in a major-power conflict.

Australia would also be a logical target for Chinese nuclear attacks, given the presence of joint US–Australia defence and intelligence facilities such as Pine Gap. Indeed, in May 2021 China's state-owned newspaper *Global Times* threatened missile strikes against Australia should Canberra work with Washington in a Taiwan contingency.

During the Cold War, it was estimated that Soviet strikes targeting the joint facilities would kill 1 million people instantly, with another 750,000 Sydneysiders perishing from radiation poisoning.

Yet Australia's leaders display a curious nonchalance, bordering at times on neglect, regarding the risks of a Taiwan conflict. In a November 2021 interview with journalist Troy Bramston, defence minister Peter Dutton said it would be "inconceivable" for Australia not to support America in defending Taiwan, with no acknowledgement of how catastrophic conflict could be. This was not the first time. During an April 2021 interview on the ABC's current affairs show *Insiders,* Dutton remarked almost blithely that "people need to be realistic" about the prospects for such a conflict. Within days, in an Anzac Day message to staff, home affairs secretary Mike Pezzullo invoked almost Churchillian rhetoric, warning of "the beating drums" of war and the prospect of Australia "send[ing] off, yet again, our warriors to fight". The following month, Prime Minister Scott Morrison fumbled his brief completely, stating during a radio interview that Australia accepts China's preferred "one country, two systems" formula for resolving this flashpoint.

Rather than admit this error, Morrison and his government just banged the war drums louder. In a joint statement following the September 2021 Australia–US Ministerial Consultations (AUSMIN), Dutton, foreign minister Marise Payne and their US counterparts used unprecedented language, emphasising "Taiwan's important role in the Indo-Pacific" and stating "their intent to strengthen ties with Taiwan, which is a leading democracy and a critical partner for both countries". The new AUKUS security partnership between Australia, the United Kingdom and the US, announced only a day prior, sent a similar message. As the respected foreign policy commentators Natasha Kassam and Darren Lim observed,

It is not in Australia's interests to push the region to the brink of the unthinkable. But let's be clear. It would also not be in Australia's interests if Taiwan, a flourishing and free democracy of 24 million people, was invaded and subjugated by force. Canberra must therefore do what it can to prevent both outcomes. AUKUS represents a judgement, a gamble even, that increasing Australia's capabilities is essential to securing a regional order favourable to its interests.

But the promised eight nuclear-powered submarines at the heart of AUKUS will play no role whatsoever in a Taiwan contingency. By the time they hit the water, most likely in the 2040s, Taiwan's fate will have been sealed. Should conflict erupt before then, Australia will be expected to contribute. If this was ever in doubt, AUKUS makes that contribution virtually automatic. Canberra's contribution would consist primarily of air and naval assets: submarines to assist with blockading the narrow South China Sea "choke points" through which Beijing's energy imports flow, alongside a combination of maritime patrol and surveillance, electronic warfare, Airborne Warning and Control System

(AWACS) and, possibly, fighter aircraft. Given the force's small size, this contribution will be purely symbolic. It will play no role in deciding the outcome of a devastating Taiwan conflict.

Australia could further explore options for shielding itself from attack during such a conflict, though there are currently no clear solutions. Serious strategic thinkers, such as former prime minister Kevin Rudd and current director of the Office of National Intelligence (ONI) Andrew Shearer, have previously called for Canberra to develop missile defences to protect the continent against Chinese and North Korean strikes. But such systems cost billions. Their reliability against China's growing arsenal of increasingly speedy and manoeuvrable missiles is also questionable. In mid-2021, for instance, Beijing reportedly caught Washington off guard when it tested a new hypersonic missile that circled the globe and can seemingly evade US missile defence systems.

Canberra could make a far bigger contribution on the diplomatic front, reducing the risk of a war that will have no winners. Australia has been here before, during the Taiwan Strait crisis of 1954–55. At one of the Cold War's most dangerous moments, when the Eisenhower administration threatened to use tactical nuclear weapons in Taiwan's defence, Prime Minister Robert Menzies lobbied vigorously for a diplomatic solution. He did so primarily through his high-level connections in Washington. But Menzies also worked with other like-minded governments in London, Ottawa and Wellington.

Morrison's mishandling of Australia's relationship with China, epitomised by his government's ham-fisted call for an independent inquiry into the origins of COVID-19, remains an obstacle. A high-level diplomatic channel to Beijing would significantly enhance Canberra's capacity to influence this flashpoint. Two decades prior to the normalisation of Sino–Australian relations, however, Menzies had no such access either. Like Australia's longest-serving prime minister, those in Canberra today could work in tandem with other middle powers in Asia – such as Japan, Singapore, South Korea and Indonesia – which have as much, if not more, to lose from a full-blown Taiwan conflict.

Better communication mechanisms to reduce the chance of crises and, most importantly, to manage the risks in a conflict of wormhole escalation are badly needed. Such measures, where they currently exist, are either inadequate or underutilised. The handful that operate between America and China are at the military-to-military level. Yet history shows that the management of major crises takes place at the civilian and civilian-to-military levels. China agreed to set up a cross-Strait hotline with Taiwan in November 2015, but has refused to answer it during Tsai's presidency due to her party's pro-independence leanings.

Critics will contend that China either can't be trusted or won't comply. But on that, the jury is still out

There is a rich agenda for Australia and its regional partners to work on. They might begin with a stocktake of crisis management and avoidance mechanisms across Asia, assessing whether these require updating and championing those which remain relevant but underutilised, such as the cross-Strait hotline. They should develop and propose new initiatives, especially in the cyber domain, where crisis management and avoidance mechanisms are desperately needed but next to non-existent. For example, they could suggest new regional rules that govern how cyber technologies should and shouldn't be used for military purposes. Asia's "alphabet soup" of multilateral organisations offers the perfect setting for advancing this agenda, particularly the Asia-Pacific Economic Cooperation (APEC) process, which Australia inspired in the late 1980s and in which Taiwan participates as "Chinese Taipei". Alternatively, Canberra could dispatch a high-level envoy – such as a serving or former senior official – to key Asian capitals to both gauge interest in and build regional support.

Critics will contend that China either can't be trusted or won't comply. But on that, the jury is still out. While it is true that Beijing refuses to pick up the cross-Strait hotline, it does use such measures when it suits. In late December 2020, for instance, when Beijing feared a US military strike during those surreal final stanzas of the erratic Trump administration, it requested a call from the chairman of the US Joint Chiefs of Staff, General Mark Milley, to confirm that such an attack wasn't imminent. Even authoritarian governments can be convinced to use crisis communication mechanisms. Soviet behaviour during the Cold War confirms this. In the wake of that conflict's most dangerous episode, the Cuban Missile Crisis of October 1962, Moscow and Washington agreed to establish a hotline connecting the Kremlin and the Pentagon. They went on to use this so-called "Direct

Communications Link" during several key moments of crisis, including to reduce the risk of US–Soviet escalation in the Arab–Israeli War of 1967.

During another of history's most harrowing conflicts, World War I, Germany's former chancellor Prince von Bülow famously asked his successor, "How did it all happen?" Chancellor Bethmann Hollweg replied, "Ah, if only we knew." But if and when a devastating Taiwan conflict erupts, there will be no excuse for ignorance. The horrendous costs and growing risks of such a conflagration are already clear and present. Moreover, the Australian public wants no part of it. In the June 2021 Lowy Institute Poll, 57 per cent of respondents said Australia should remain neutral in a US–China military conflict. Rather than beating the war drums, Canberra should instead be working much harder to head off this coming calamity. The time for diplomacy is now. ∎

FREEDOM CRY

The view from Taiwan

Yu-Jie Chen

What do we talk about when we talk about Taiwan? In international policy discussions, Taiwan is often described as a "question", a "problem" or, even more melodramatically, "trouble". In such narratives, Taiwan is seen as needing to be dealt with, and the agency of the island's 23.4 million people is sidelined, if not overlooked. Therefore, the title of this issue – *The Taiwan Choice* – is refreshing, assuming that it also includes Taiwan's own choice. After all, as other countries are debating what decisions they should make about Taiwan, Taiwanese people will be making their own decisions as well, for themselves.

Indeed, the people of Taiwan have become well-practised in exercising their freedom of choice since its democratisation in the 1980s. Today, facing China's increasingly bellicose threats, Taiwanese are choosing not to bow to the pressure and to continue their democratic way of life.

But such freedom has been a scarce resource for people on Taiwan throughout most of its history. The indigenous population of the island known as Formosa ("Beautiful Island") did not have much choice when Han immigrants from the mainland took their lands. The later Taiwanese population, consisting of aboriginal peoples and the Hoklo and Hakka of the Han people, did not have much choice when the Dutch and Spanish briefly colonised parts of the island. They also did not have a choice when the Chinese Qing Dynasty incorporated Taiwan into the Manchu regime and then, after its defeat in the First Sino–Japanese War of 1894–95, ceded Taiwan's sovereignty to Japan. Nor did they have a choice when the Allied powers after World War II handed Taiwan and its outlying Pescadores Islands (P'eng-hu) to Generalissimo Chiang Kai-shek of the Nationalist Party (KMT). They had no choice when Chiang's Republic of China (ROC) government massacred tens of thousands of Taiwanese in the 228 Incident of 1947 and inflicted "White Terror" on Taiwan during the following decades.

Nevertheless, Taiwanese persisted. Even in the darkest days, when the KMT imposed what was then the longest period of martial law in history (1949–87), Taiwanese – including those who had migrated from mainland China with Chiang's troops around 1949 – sought freedom wherever they could, wrestling civil, political, and labour rights from the government through some of the most sophisticated grassroots movements ever seen this side of the Pacific. These courageous efforts of previous generations led to Taiwan's transformation from an authoritarian regime to a young democracy, in which we have agency by engaging in political debate, casting our votes and making our voices heard – all without fear of retaliation from the government in power.

Tense ties with China

While the story of Taiwan's domestic affairs is one of increasing democratisation and individual autonomy, the road to "international emancipation" has been more fraught. This complexity starts close to home. Taiwan's seventy-plus-year relationship with the People's Republic of China (PRC or China) has been complicated, to put it mildly. From military skirmishes between the 1950s and 1970s to gradual, tentative contact in the 1980s and 1990s, to the present-day political stalemate, it has never been easy to navigate relations across the Taiwan Strait, even though cooperation was made possible after Taiwan's democratisation.

During the 1990s, Taipei–Beijing relations had ups and downs. There were initial, sporadic displays of reconciliation, such as the negotiations in 1992 to enable cross-Strait arrangements on practical matters such as tracing registered mail. But just getting to the negotiating table required diplomatic innovation. The PRC and the ROC, which still did not recognise each other, were reluctant to officially cooperate. To resolve this issue, both governments established nominally non-governmental institutions to act as proxies – often called "white-glove" organisations. In March 1991, Taiwan established the Straits Exchange Foundation (SEF), a government-funded non-profit organisation. In December that year, SEF's counterpart in mainland China – the Association for Relations Across the Taiwan Straits – was created. The two organisations are authorised by their governments to contact each other and negotiate, and to conclude and implement cross-Strait agreements. In 1993, talks between these proxy organisations led to the signing of four agreements, one of the first instances of Taipei–Beijing cooperation.

This limited progress, however, was interrupted in 1995 when Taiwan's then president, Lee Teng-hui (1988–2000), visited Cornell University. There, at his alma mater, he gave a consequential speech about Taiwan's democratisation and introduced a new political term, "ROC on Taiwan". This term implied not only that the ROC ruled Taiwan and Taiwan only – demonstrating plainly that the ROC does not rule in China – but also that the ROC government was elected by Taiwanese and Taiwanese only. The PRC government was infuriated.

Beijing was further enraged in 1999 when Lee, as Taiwan's first democratically elected leader, defined cross-Strait relations as "special state-to-state" relations. Years later, Lee's successor, Chen Shui-bian of the Democratic Progressive Party (DPP), would, in a similar effort, coin the phrase "one country on each side [of the Strait]" to refer to Taiwan's independent status. From Beijing's perspective, these were both attempts to separate Taiwan from the PRC.

The movement demonstrated a growing Taiwanese national identity, forged over generations

As a result, the Chinese Communist Party (CCP) was keen to find a political ally in Taiwan. Many politicians in the KMT, a party established on the mainland when the ROC was founded in 1912, are ideologically and sentimentally tied to China. On the other hand, many in the DPP have seen KMT governments as émigré regimes that are obstacles to Taiwan's autonomy. The KMT and the DPP, since the founding of the latter in 1986, have competed fiercely, especially over Taiwan's relationship with China: the KMT insists that Taiwan is part of China (although the KMT's "China" is the Republic of China, not the People's Republic of China), while the DPP holds that Taiwan is not part of China/PRC and should not claim to represent "China" at all on the world stage.

As a result, when the KMT's Ma Ying-jeou was elected president in 2008, the CCP and the KMT shared an agenda to deter what they saw as the growth of "Taiwan independence" that Chen Shui-bian's rule (2000–2008) had encouraged. From 2008 to 2016, when Ma was in office, Taipei and Beijing – through their proxy organisations and party-to-party forums – signed twenty-three cross-Strait agreements in multiple areas, including transportation, tourism, judicial assistance, and trade and investment.

Yet the opaque way in which these negotiations were conducted, compounded by the KMT's aggressive pushing of the agreements through Taiwan's legislature, agitated many Taiwanese, especially young people anxious about closer ties with Beijing. This democratic deficit was a prologue to the landmark 2014 Sunflower Movement, in which Taiwanese students stormed into and occupied the legislative chamber for twenty-four days. In support, an unprecedented half a million people took to the streets in a peaceful protest.

That movement put a dampener on CCP–KMT cooperation and halted any new agreements. Even a history-making meeting between Xi Jinping and Ma Ying-jeou in 2015 in Singapore was not able to rekindle cross-Strait relations, especially as the KMT was about to lose its presidential platform.

Taiwanese identity

When a dispute drags on for decades, its underlying nature can change with each generation. Just as Taiwanese have chosen a different domestic social contract to that in China, they also desire a different relationship with China, one that is not dictated by the continuing influence of the past authoritarian regime under Chiang Kai-shek or his heir, Chiang Ching-kuo, both of whom unrealistically pledged to "recover the mainland" after their KMT had fled mainland China in 1949. The Sunflower Movement's pushback reflects not only a widespread outlook in Taiwan that refuses political absorption by China but a rejection of the sentimentality – common among older KMT members – that cooperation, or even some kind of integration, with the mainland is a necessary denouement to the saga of cross-Strait separation. Instead, the movement demonstrated a growing Taiwanese national identity, forged over generations. This evolving identity has been a political boon for the DPP. It helped Tsai Ing-wen of the DPP secure two landslide victories, in the 2016 and 2020 presidential elections, and has given the DPP legislative majorities since 2016.

This increasing aversion to closer links with China is also clear from various polls. A survey by the National Chengchi University's Election Study Center on stances on unification and independence since 1994 has steadily demonstrated that people in Taiwan favour the "status quo". For many Taiwanese, the "status quo" is essentially code for the independence we currently enjoy. However, the status quo is also a kind of coerced choice, made with an awareness that if Taiwan declares a desire to unequivocally separate from China, it will likely suffer an attack by the People's Liberation Army. As of December 2021, 55 per cent of the Taiwanese population preferred to maintain the status quo, which included 28 per cent who wished to "decide at a later date" and 27 per cent who wanted to maintain the status quo "indefinitely".

But the past few years have witnessed an unusually swift opinion shift. Since 2018, support for "independence" has climbed quickly, while the already low support for unification with China has plummeted. The two most notable changes were in the position of "move toward independence (while maintaining the status quo in the meantime)", which rose from 15 per cent support in 2018 to 25 per cent in December 2021, and the position of "move toward unification (while maintaining the status quo in the meantime),", which fell precipitously from 13 per cent support in 2018 to 6 per cent in December 2021.

Another survey by the same centre is similarly insightful. It asked people whether they identify as "Taiwanese", "both Taiwanese and Chinese", or "Chinese". The trend is clear: a Taiwanese-only identity is becoming the norm. As of December 2021, 62 per cent of people in Taiwan identified as exclusively "Taiwanese", up from 55 per cent in 2018. People who identify as "both Taiwanese and Chinese" dropped to 32 per cent, one of its lowest levels since 1992, while those identifying as exclusively "Chinese" remained a low 3 per cent.

These surveys suggest a steady, long-term shift by Taiwanese away from ever wanting to unite with China. China's unpopularity has likely been enhanced by events in Hong Kong since June 2019. Taiwanese closely observed these events and understood their implications in a way few other nations could. They watched the fierce street protests, mostly peaceful, by millions of Hong Kongers in that hot summer and the continued resistance through the autumn. They witnessed the Hong Kong government's violent suppression of protesters, including the widespread police brutality and over 16,000 rounds of tear gas permeating the city. They also saw Beijing's harsh reaction, especially the stunning imposition of the national security law for Hong Kong, which brooks no political dissent.

This democracy is all that most young Taiwanese have ever known

Taiwanese were used to protests in their own streets, but the contrast between their government's response to dissent and that of the Hong Kong government spoke volumes, and triggered memories of Beijing's 1989 Tiananmen Square massacre. It prompted further sympathy for Hong Kong's democratic movement and antipathy towards

China's "One Country, Two Systems" formula, which was originally designed for Taiwan in 1981 by Deng Xiaoping and later applied to Hong Kong and Macau.

Moreover, many in Taiwan have been put off, even repelled, by Xi Jinping's aggressive unification agenda. Of particular note was his January 2019 speech marking the fortieth anniversary of the PRC's "Message to Compatriots in Taiwan", in which Xi advanced One Country, Two Systems as the "best approach" to unify Taiwan with the mainland. While calling for a peaceful transition, he made it clear that China may use force, at its discretion, to achieve unification.

Naturally, the prospect of unification through threats or use of force alienated the already apprehensive Taiwan society, and Xi's mention of One Country, Two Systems was poorly timed, given what Taiwanese would later see as a terrifying application of the formula in Hong Kong. President Tsai Ing-wen responded swiftly and firmly, emphasising that her government has never accepted that Taiwan is part of China. Xi's speech was so unpalatable in Taiwan that it even elicited a response from the KMT, which confirmed that the ROC is an independent, sovereign state and that Xi's One Country, Two Systems cannot at this stage win the majority support of Taiwanese.

These developments have precipitated a rare convergence in Taiwan's domestic politics: people in Taiwan, as well as the two leading parties, have formed a consensus that favours their nation continuing as a democratic, sovereign state in which they can sustain their democratic way of life.

The independence myth

Through individual and collective choices, large and small, Taiwanese have built a thriving, modern democracy with hard-won civil and political freedoms. This democracy is all that most young Taiwanese have ever known.

Taiwan (including its offshore P'eng-hu, Quemoy and Matsu islands) has never been ruled by the PRC. For more than seven decades, Taiwan has had a government called the Republic of China; it has an autonomous, liberal democratic system entirely different from China's one-party state; and it has the capacity to engage in foreign relations (albeit often under significant restraints imposed by Beijing through its international influence). For most Taiwanese, this is bona fide independence as we know and live it.

Taiwan's formal international legal status, on the other hand, is more fraught. Much ink has been spilled over this subject, and the focus of this essay does not allow for elaboration. It suffices to note that Taiwan meets all qualifications of statehood under the Montevideo Convention on the Rights and Duties of States; that is, it has a permanent population, a defined territory, a government and the capacity to enter into relations with other states.

What burdens Taiwan's statehood are two major questions.

The first question concerns diplomatic recognition. While most international law scholars do not regard recognition as a requirement of statehood, some argue that Taiwan's relative lack of diplomatic recognition in the international community undermines its statehood.

This view, however, is misguided, because recognition is the result of intergovernmental, political negotiations, rather than of international legal capacity (statehood). While most states do not recognise Taiwan because of pressure from China, Taiwan is able to maintain informal relations with many countries on all matters except in name (think of Taiwan's relationship with the United States and Japan, for example), and Taiwan has formal diplomatic relations with a small number of countries.

The second question is its relationship with mainland China. Some scholars have claimed that because Taiwan has not unequivocally asserted its separation from China, it cannot be recognised as a state distinct from China. This view fails to acknowledge that the PRC consistently threatens to use force if the ROC on Taiwan chooses to have its sovereignty recognised internationally. Taiwanese prefer the independence they already enjoy to Taiwan being destroyed. What would be the point of being recognised as a state if the state was shattered by war to begin with? There is also little gain for Taiwan in "declaring separation" – at this juncture, most countries would not support what they would see as a provocative action by Taiwan.

Indeed, the myth that Taiwan has to declare what it already has is misguided – the ROC constitution was amended in 1991 to reflect that the government only controls Taiwan, P'eng-hu, Quemoy and Matsu, not the mainland (it was meant to "tailor the suit to the size of Taiwan", according to one of the participants in the amendment process); Taiwan's president and legislature are directly elected by the

Taiwanese people only; Taiwanese continually exercise their rights and freedoms in a democratic society, all without the PRC's involvement. This is the embodiment of self-determination.

Taiwan's independence is a lived history and a living reality. This was why Lee Teng-hui called the nation the "ROC on Taiwan" in 1995. This was also why, in 1999, the DPP incorporated the "Resolution on Taiwan's Future" into the party's charter, according to which Taiwan is already a democratic, independent country under the name of the Republic of China. Any change to "Taiwan's independent status quo" must be decided by all residents of Taiwan through a referendum.

If Taiwan's independence from China were not plain enough, President Tsai Ing-wen's 2019 National Day speech confirmed it. She emphasised that the Taiwanese people have together experienced a seventy-year journey and have

The 1992 Consensus was actually a dissensus on the question of "one China"

forged shared memories. She used the term "Republic of China (Taiwan)" for the first time. Slightly, yet significantly, different from Lee's "ROC on Taiwan" nomenclature, "ROC (Taiwan)" further intertwines the ROC with Taiwan.

Her speech resonated with most Taiwanese because it reflected their reality on the ground: the ROC is Taiwan and Taiwan is the ROC. People in Taiwan are bound by their collective choices over the past seventy years, including building a constitutional democracy. Their three generations of memories are distinct from those of people on the mainland, and they have fashioned an independent body politic.

The spell of "one China"

Then why is the ROC (Taiwan), which functions as an independent sovereign state, still confronted with immense difficulties in its relations with the PRC and other countries? The obvious answer is Beijing's strict insistence that the whole world, including Taiwan, should abide by its "One China principle", which essentially asserts that Taiwan is "an inseparable part" of the PRC's territory.

Some states disagree. They do not accept Beijing's claim that Taiwan is part of the PRC. The notable example is the United States, which has its own "One China policy" to differentiate its position from the PRC's. According to this policy, Washington takes note of Beijing's position that Taiwan is part of China, but has made it clear that the United States is neutral on the question of Taiwan's sovereignty and that any dispute should be resolved peacefully.

Hence, the question for the ROC (Taiwan) is not whether to declare independence from China but how to reject Beijing's "One China principle" without giving the PRC an excuse to start a war. The KMT attempted a version of this during Ma Ying-jeou's rule. It coined what has become known as the "1992 Consensus", which the party claimed resulted from the brief exchanges during the 1992 negotiations between the two governments' proxies. Based on the 1992

Consensus, the KMT was able to cooperate on economic fronts with the PRC between 2008 and 2016.

Just as the classic ambiguous illustration of the duck–rabbit blurs boundaries between perception and interpretation, the 1992 Consensus was intended by the KMT as an illusion, connoting different meanings for the KMT and the CCP. The KMT used it to refer to its own formula of "One China, Respective Interpretations", in which "China" referred to the Republic of China. But, to the CCP, "China" of course means the People's Republic of China. The KMT acknowledged that the CCP had a different interpretation of "China". Yet, Beijing has never acknowledged the KMT's formula.

The 1992 Consensus was actually a dissensus on the question of "one China", but it provided a convenient cover at a time when the two parties were eager to cooperate. Neither the KMT nor the CCP wished to publicly challenge the other's rhetoric. In essence, the 1992 Consensus was a diplomatic manoeuvre to feign unison while avoiding confrontation.

Its intentional ambiguity worked at the time, but it was also confusing to the Taiwanese public. In a 2019 survey, more than 80 per cent of Taiwanese did not accept the 1992 Consensus being defined as "One China (PRC)" without acknowledging the existence of the ROC. There are also diverse understandings of what the 1992 Consensus even means: as many as 44 per cent of Taiwanese think that it refers to "the two sides of the Strait being two separate countries".

Whatever the proper understanding of the 1992 Consensus, its original illusion no longer seems to satisfy Beijing or Taipei. From the DPP government's perspective, the KMT's word play smuggles the idea of "one China" into Taiwan. The DPP rejects that there has ever been a 1992 Consensus, and it refuses any notion that Taiwan is part of China. In the meantime, Xi Jinping's CCP has pushed One Country, Two Systems, building on its interpretation of the 1992 Consensus. This has put the KMT into a bind, as it undercuts the strategic ambiguity intended by the original formulation. The more Xi presses for unification, the less the KMT can sell any "one China" stances to Taiwan voters and maintain the veneer of the 1992 Consensus as a harmonious consensus. Moreover, with the threat of China's increasing military activities around the island, any "one China" notion will further lose its already limited appeal in Taiwan.

The future of Taiwan

This is not to say there is no room for Beijing–Taipei cooperation. If – and this is a big if – Beijing is willing to set aside One Country, Two Systems and accept the ambiguity of whatever formula the two sides can agree on, there will be an opportunity to reduce tension and resume contact.

But China is taking the opposite approach. The People's Liberation Army has been penetrating Taiwan's air defence identification zone with unprecedented frequency. Its aircraft carriers have led naval drills off Taiwan. It has also held amphibious-assault and island-control exercises that focus on Taiwan. The circumstances are so tense that *The Economist* published a headline last year that referred to Taiwan as "the most dangerous place on Earth".

I am often asked how we in Taiwan react to this perilous situation. The Taiwanese people are not panicking. After all, generations of Taiwanese have lived under China's military threats. Many Taiwanese believe that Beijing is using this tactic to engender fear, a kind of PSYOP muscle-flexing. A recent survey shows that almost two-thirds of Taiwanese do not believe that "sooner or later, the CCP will ultimately invade Taiwan". As to whether Taiwanese are willing to defend their country if worst comes to worst, polls point to different results. Taiwan's Foundation for Democracy found that almost 80 per cent of Taiwanese were willing to fight for Taiwan. In a poll conducted by Duke University that had more open-ended questions, however, only 23 per cent were prepared to commit acts of resistance.

Taiwan's democracy is a rare success story in the Indo-Pacific region

But Taiwanese cannot afford to succumb to the numbing effects of Beijing's constant scare tactics. We should do more to bolster our own asymmetrical defence capabilities. President Tsai Ing-wen has announced plans to establish the All-Out Defense Mobilization Agency in 2022 to reform the military and prepare Taiwan's reserve force as a back-up. The government should also organise and ready the civilian response to hold out as long as possible until international aid, if any, arrives.

In addition, Taiwan needs unity. Political competition is normal in a dynamic democracy, but facing a potential invader, all parties in Taiwan should come together to defend the island. The KMT and the DPP have more in common than they would like to admit: both view our nation as a democratic, sovereign state, and both reject One Country, Two Systems. A healthy democracy requires not only vigorous political competition but also resilience and a united will to defend its institutions.

While Taiwan can and should do its part, it cannot do it alone. It will require support from other like-minded democracies that have the foresight to recognise that the authoritarian advances on Taiwan also represent a threat to them and their national interests. Support does not simply mean military defence during war. Peacetime support is also crucial, including helping Taiwan strengthen its economic relations with other nations so that it does not overly rely on China, and allowing greater Taiwanese participation in an international environment that has largely isolated Taiwan. The United States' invitation for Taiwan to join the Summit for Democracy was a good gesture, and Taiwan is in need of more meaningful, practicable steps, such as allowing it to join the Comprehensive and Progressive Agreement for Trans-Pacific Partnership. What is unhelpful is the kind of short-sighted view held, for example, by former Australian prime minister Paul Keating, who said last November that Taiwan was "not a vital Australian interest" and labelled it a "civil matter" for China.

How wrong he was. Taiwan stands on the front lines of China's belligerence and is not just a territory it wishes to absorb – Taiwan signifies a counter-narrative that the CCP is determined to erase. Taiwan's democracy is a rare success story in the Indo-Pacific region, undermining China's claims to its own people that the democratic age is coming to an end and that its political model is superior. Taiwan's per-capita income is among the highest in the world; it provides a competing development model to China's state capitalism, which disrespects democratic values and human rights but is rapidly winning converts throughout the developing world. Taiwan has produced technological innovation and sophistication that China is yet to attain and desperately desires. Home of the world's most valuable chipmaker, Taiwan is vital to the electronics and high-tech supply chains that fuel global technological and economic growth. Taiwan's vibrant democracy, its prosperity and its technological dynamism are more critical than many realise to the success of the democratic project and the continuation of the international economic order as we know it. These achievements are also the shared inheritance of 23 million Taiwanese – a hard-won birthright that we will continue to defend.

Taiwan's choice is increasingly clear: the Taiwanese people want what they already have – to continue the democratic self-rule that has provided economic prosperity without compromising human dignity. They want to be able to decide their own future, just as people in other liberal democracies do. What about the rest of the world? What is your Taiwan choice? ■

This essay is in memory of Chih-Yi Cameron Chen, who is dearly remembered as a beloved friend.

YOUNG GUNS

Is a generation gap fuelling Australia's China debate?

Stephen Dziedzic

Deep in the bowels of one of Canberra's sprawling government departments, a young man beavers away each day on Australia's foreign policy. I can't identify him, because he's not meant to speak to the media. He does not hold a senior position, but he's bright – if he decides to stick with life in the public service, there's every chance he could ascend to the commanding heights of the bureaucracy.

We meet in a nondescript park not far from the rather bland edifice which houses his office (or rather, his desk) and sip our takeaway coffees.

I'm speaking to him because I want him to help answer a question which has nagged at me for quite some time: is there a generational divide reshaping China policy in Canberra?

In brief, the narrative of a generational shift runs like this. Australia's policy towards China has changed dramatically since late 2017, when Malcolm Turnbull's government announced foreign interference laws and then blocked Chinese telco Huawei from Australia's 5G networks. And this change has, in part, been driven by an emerging generation of younger politicians, analysts and public servants who are deeply suspicious about the intentions and trajectory of the Chinese Communist Party, who have emphasised Australian sovereignty over accommodation, and who have championed a markedly hawkish set of policies towards Beijing.

The young public servant looks at me carefully. He wants to stress the limits of his power. He is a small cog in a huge, whirring machine. Decisions are made by politicians, not public servants.

But that doesn't mean the assumptions and ideas about China which flow through the major departments in Canberra – Foreign Affairs and Trade, Defence, the intelligence agencies or Prime Minister and Cabinet – don't matter.

And when our man assesses his friends and colleagues – largely millennial or gen-Z officials and staffers starting to work their way through the ranks, eyes fixed hopefully on the glittering prizes in the upper echelons of politics and the public service – he sees a striking conformity of views on Beijing.

"If you look at my organisation, across many of these [departments] and speak to people who are in their twenties and thirties, or even forties, what is really clear is that there is a clear realisation about what China is, and what it's becoming," he says. "And then over the course of the last couple of years what you've seen is a real hardening of attitudes again, largely because of what [China] has been doing. This hasn't come out of the blue. The aggressive language, their actions in places like Hong Kong, the trade strikes [on Australia] – it's all had an impact."

Of course, this shift isn't limited to younger Australians or to policymakers in Canberra. The sharp and rapid deterioration of the bilateral relationship – itself driven by Beijing's campaign of economic coercion against Australia – has resulted in growing public distrust of China and its leaders. That distrust has fed into offices, homes and chat groups across Australia, not just into the Cabinet room or the departmental conference rooms on the upper floors of Russell and R.G. Casey.

But our public servant sees a particular intensity and near-uniformity of views among the emerging generation of foreign policy practitioners, analysts and political operators in Canberra, where being "clear-eyed" about China is now a prerequisite for being dealt into the game, even at the margins.

"It's become a marker of your seriousness," he tells me.

"You either get China or you don't. And if you get it, that means you understand the threat posed ... and have a really clear-eyed understanding of what it means for Australia and what we have to do in turn."

History didn't end after all

Let's get an important caveat out of the way. Generalisations about generations always risk obscuring more than they reveal, and it takes little effort to find glaring exceptions. Indeed, some of the most visible and influential China hawks in Canberra are baby boomers, not twenty-something tearaways, and the actual decision-makers who have shaped Australia's China policy – from ministers through to senior officials – are men and women at the peak of their careers, often in their forties, fifties and sixties.

But if our public servant is right, and a cohort of politicians, officials, journalists and analysts in their twenties, thirties and forties have backed, pushed along and cheered on this rapid shift, then it's worth assessing what might be driving them.

The former director-general of the Office of National Assessments (ONA), Allan Gyngell – who keeps a close eye on Australian foreign policy – thinks there is only a "glimmer of truth" to the argument that

Canberra's younger generation ... [sees] a country which has gone terribly awry

there's a generational split on China policy in Canberra. Still, he agrees that the arc traced by China over the last three or four decades – roughly the lifespan of the generation we are talking about – has shaped the attitudes of younger policymakers and analysts.

"Each generation of policymakers has a different China in the back of their minds when they are thinking about it. And that is inevitably shaped by the China they know and the China they've seen," he tells me.

And for some younger Australians, two different Chinas loom, almost as mirror images: the nation we thought it would be, and the nation it is today.

Many Australians in their thirties came to political consciousness in the sunlit uplands of the 1990s, during what now looks like a fleeting unipolar moment of American pre-eminence. I was born in 1983, and one of my earlier memories is of the Berlin Wall coming down; what I remember most keenly is not the image of the sledgehammers hitting the concrete, but the unusual intensity in my dad's voice as he sat me down in front of the TV news bulletin and told me to watch.

The political universe which slowly formed in my mind was ordered, and its trajectory was clear. The United States was ascendant, democracy was on the march, and the great civilising flows of capital streaming through the world would soon transform and liberalise autocracies and developing countries – including, of course, China.

This was my first view of the behemoth, and it loomed not as a threat, but as a land of promise. Beijing had steadily normalised its relationships with a host of countries, opened its economy and was now knocking on the doors of the World Trade Organization (WTO). It seemed almost certain to slowly liberalise (if not democratise) as its newly prosperous middle class demanded the freedoms enjoyed in the West.

Was this worldview a caricature? Of course. Was it laughably naive? Probably. But people older and smarter than me were making similarly cosy assumptions, and while those expectations have now been well and truly shattered – not least by a China which grew rich and powerful without becoming free – some of these ideas have shaped attitudes towards Beijing among young and old alike.

And often, when Canberra's younger generation looks at the China of 2022 – powerful, bellicose, revanchist, illiberal – they see a country which has gone terribly awry from what they expected. This can feed a sense of anxiety and distrust.

"There is probably a nagging sense [with China] of 'it wasn't meant to be like this,'" one younger federal parliamentarian tells me. "We're probably projecting a lot of our own expectations, but there is still a sense that China was on one path which was comforting and familiar and now it's headed off in a direction very unfamiliar to us, and which worries us deeply. And, of course, if you look what it's doing both internally and externally, then those worries are largely justified."

Older generations might share some of these anxieties, but they often don't have the same sense of jolted dislocation. From Gyngell's vantage point, for example, Zhao Lijian and other wolf warriors berating Beijing's enemies from their podiums and social media accounts don't look like strange new beasts, but are echoes of the China he encountered as a young official. "For me, the China I begin with is the China of Mao and the Cultural Revolution. When I was first posted [as an Australian diplomat] in 1970, we were not allowed to talk with Chinese diplomats. Australia didn't recognise China, and its people abroad were all clad in Mao suits talking to each other in the corner of diplomatic receptions," he says. "If you grew up in the nineties, that wouldn't be so apparent. China was more like the established countries around us. You were not quite as aware of that history."

Younger China watchers in Canberra might bridle at that. They might not have been alive when China was roiled by the Cultural Revolution, but many have read the history closely and say they're perfectly equipped to see China's contemporary politics in context.

That said, if you examine the backgrounds of many younger China watchers and professionals in Canberra today, they often trace a similar journey – from curiosity to fascination, to deep engagement, and then to unease and, finally, disillusionment.

Many started off simply as smart teenagers who realised quite early that China would be a big story this century, and were drawn into its orbit because it was intellectually fascinating, increasingly consequential or a lucrative market. Potentially all three.

Fergus Ryan, an analyst for the Australian Strategic Policy Institute, who has written extensively about Chinese technology and censorship, was one of those who kept going back to China as it boomed, opened up to the world and took tentative steps towards liberalisation. He spent several years studying and working in the country, learning the language and finding his feet in the corporate sector, even working for one of China's biggest film stars, Li Bingbing.

He says those years gave him a ringside seat – and a sharper understanding of both the magnitude and speed of the changes in China since around 2010: the crackdowns on civil society, the closing of public spaces, the wolf-warrior diplomacy, the growing suspicion of outsiders.

"I think my trajectory is quite common," Ryan tells me.

"I started off quite hopeful, and the China that I knew when I was first going over there was much more open in the Hu Jintao era. It was really exciting to open up a Weibo account for the first time and read opinions on there and look at the debate. But then, slowly but surely, over time – and this accelerated when Xi [Jinping] came to power – that civic space just shank and shrank and shrank."

Keating's barbs

It's not easy to find dissenting voices on China in Canberra. The widespread anxiety about the way the Chinese nation has changed under Xi Jinping – its increasingly aggressive behaviour towards neighbouring countries, its economic coercion – has helped to harden something like a consensus: Australia cannot yield.

Yes, there have been some furious altercations. The shadow foreign minister, Penny Wong, has made scorching criticisms of the government's handling of the relationship, accusing it of deliberately stoking the prospect of war over Taiwan in a crude attempt to win votes. The defence minister, Peter Dutton, responded by accusing Labor of trying to abandon the US alliance. But the reality is that the ALP is largely in lock step with the government's policies on China, supporting the decision to lock out Huawei, the condemnation of China's human rights abuses, the crackdown on foreign investment, the scrutiny of research collaboration and the passage of foreign interference laws.

Many of the most vocal critics of the Coalition's shift in China policy have now left government entirely. This group includes some distinguished figures who occupied the heights of public life in the nineties or the noughts, and who worked to substantially deepen ties with Beijing.

The most prominent of these critics has been former Labor prime minister Paul Keating, who championed engagement with Asia when in power and has mounted a furious campaign against the current government's policies, accusing Scott Morrison and his lieutenants of needlessly provoking China at the behest of the United States. In Keating's view, Australia's current policies on China are not really about China at all, but about us. They're the rotten fruit borne of our own insecurity and our profound sense of isolation in Asia, flecked with racist suspicion and a barely concealed longing for the era when our Anglosphere cousins – the United States and, before her, the United Kingdom – ruled the waves.

"Twenty per cent of humanity drags themselves out of poverty and we say, 'No, no, no, this is not right, you have to stay in the mud. Know your place, you have to stay down there in the mud,'" Keating told the National Press Club in November. He declared that China was not intent on overturning the existing international order or institutions but merely wanted to reshape them in ways that accommodate its interests. He also brushed off questions about China's threats to Taiwan, its militarisation of the South China Sea and increasingly hostile diplomacy, saying the country was simply in "the adolescent phase of their diplomacy" with "testosterone running everywhere".

But to many younger Australian analysts and MPs, this is a picture of China set in aspic, and little more than a reformulation of the conclusions Keating drew about Beijing in the 1990s.

"At least we have come to terms with what's happened [in China]," one Australian MP tells me.

Some also see a touch of defensiveness. After Keating penned an opinion piece lashing the Australian media's portrayal of China and claiming that Beijing, unlike the United States, "does not attack other states", James Palmer from *Foreign Policy* observed acerbically that it would be "surprising" to the "people of India, Vietnam, Tibet and Taiwan". "Why are 1990s leaders so committed to repeating absolute bullshit talking points fed to them by the Chinese? In part it's because they absorbed them

On the face of it, Paterson and Hastie are an unusual political couple

in an era when Beijing was much more about courting than threatening," Palmer wrote on Twitter. "But it's also cognitive dissonance. They screwed up when dealing with China, vastly overestimating the benefits and liberalisation of engagement, and underestimating the ideology, authoritarianism and revanchism."

They might not put it so bluntly – after all, Keating remains a Labor legend – but some of today's Labor MPs agree. Victorian MP Peter Khalil wrote an opinion piece headlined "Why my hero Keating is wrong on China". "Embarrassing," messaged another Labor MP when asked for their view after the National Press Club speech.

Penny Wong was more measured, but there was still a hint of acid in her response when she observed that "China has changed" and suggested that Keating might benefit from contemporary advice from experts. "Obviously, as the current leadership of the party, we have the benefit of contemporary briefings about Australia's strategic circumstances. And we formulate our position based on that advice," she said.

When I ask the young public servant about Keating, he smiles awkwardly and looks almost embarrassed as he shakes his head. This is a common reflex from Canberra wonks in their twenties or thirties whenever the former PM is mentioned. They don't want to scoff openly at a giant of Australian politics, but it's hard to escape the sense that they see Keating as a figure now rather sadly untethered from reality.

"If you look hard at what China is, not what you want it to be, then it's hard not to worry," he says.

Asked if he can name anyone in his professional circles who would agree with Keating, he doesn't have to think for long.

"I can't think of anyone," he replies.

There's also the question of access. When the relationship was in good health, Australian politicians and diplomats could meet relatively easily with their counterparts. But China's decision to essentially freeze out Australian leaders in the wake of the broader collapse in ties means that many younger analysts and officials have struggled to get access to – let alone purchase on – the Chinese system.

I remember talking to another mid-level Australian official about their work on China back in 2018. This was when the relationship was deteriorating, but well before the crisis precipitated by Australia's call for an inquiry into the COVID-19 outbreak in 2020. Even then, securing phone calls for officials and ministers or gaining traction on core issues was "like banging your head repeatedly against the same brick wall," the official complained.

In contrast, some former Australian politicians and senior public servants – at least those regarded as relatively friendly by the Chinese government – still retain privileged access to decision-makers in China, or enjoy lucrative corporate gigs with Chinese companies.

Fergus Ryan doesn't dismiss the idea that millennials might be heavily influenced by what they saw on their TV sets in the 1990s, but adds: "I think most of us got China wrong."

"I think the difference between the generations is that the younger generation is now less invested in this position that China was going to liberalise with more engagement."

Gyngell insists he isn't blind to the authoritarian turn of the Chinese Communist Party under Xi. He argues that China's government needs to be seen not as a uniquely malignant threat but primarily as a great power which is determined to use the full range of tools at its disposal to influence, intimidate and deter other countries, and to reshape the world around it. "China is a big power, acting like a big power does. We have to deal with them as we would any big power," he says.

Gyngell suggests that some younger Australian decision-makers and analysts seem so fixated by China's authoritarianism that it's the chief frame of reference they use to make sense of the country. "It generates the idea of China as a super-efficient, single-minded, purposeful entity," he tells me. "And I think that blinds us – or can blind us – to the contractions and contradictions and difficulties that the system faces."

The Wolverines

If Canberra does have a new guard on China, then James Paterson is one of its most visible lieutenants. The Victorian Liberal senator is blessed (or cursed) with a fresh face, making him look even younger than his thirty-four years. But he's also been one of the government's most adroit and persistent advocates for a more assertive China policy. Last year he was appointed chair of the influential Parliamentary Joint Committee on Intelligence and Security, replacing another youngish China hawk – 39-year-old Liberal MP Andrew Hastie – who had been promoted to the outer ministry.

On the face of it, Paterson and Hastie are an unusual political couple. Paterson is agnostic, slight of frame, and precise in his language, while Hastie is a deeply religious and muscular ex–Special Forces captain, who copped flak after comparing China's rise to the West's failure to confront Nazi Germany in the 1930s.

But both men share deep convictions on foreign affairs and were founding members of the most controversial manifestation of youthful vigour and ambition on China policy: a bipartisan group of MPs and senators, all China hawks, who called themselves "the Wolverines".

The Wolverines sprang into existence in 2017, when several Liberal MPs – including Paterson and Hastie – mounted a furious internal campaign to help torpedo the Turnbull government's push to ratify a 2007 extradition treaty with China. Turnbull ultimately shelved the treaty after Labor also withdrew support.

Paterson was aghast at the prospect of ratification, convinced that Chinese authorities would use it to drag dissidents and other opponents hiding in Australia back to China, where they would face a notoriously opaque and politicised legal system.

The contest was electrifying for Paterson. He says it made him think more deeply about what sort of bargain Australia had struck with its biggest trading partner and comprehensive strategic partner, and what China expected in return.

The Morrison and Turnbull governments have ticked off many items on the Wolverines' wish list

"It was definitely the catalyst for me. It brought into sharp relief that the Australian political class was dangerously naive about the consequences of this," he tells me. "I couldn't understand why an Australian prime minister or foreign minister would do this. So I started to think about why the political class were so heavily invested in this positive idea of China, when the indicators [about its trajectory] were already so bad."

These twin assumptions – that China had turned towards authoritarianism at home and expansionism abroad, and that Australia needed a substantially different and bipartisan policy to meet that threat – motivated everything the group did.

The group was dominated by MPs in their thirties and forties. Its name was a reference to an execrable Cold War flick called *Red Dawn*, which features a group of US high-school kids – the Wolverines – who fight a daring rear-guard action to repel Soviet invaders from American soil.

The Wolverines group was sometimes breathlessly described as "secretive", but several members embraced publicity. There were double-page spreads in newspapers, a steady stream of online commentary, even stickers of claws marks stuck on some Senate office doors.

"It was absolutely generational," Paterson says. "We could only do things like that because we weren't too far along in our careers. [But] we were relaxed about the heat it generated, because we had a political task to change the debate. And the group was a handy tool in getting the message out to a larger audience."

And they set about it with gusto. Wolverines members took every opportunity to lash Beijing for human rights abuses, as well as agitating publicly and privately for new laws to tackle foreign government interference, overhaul foreign investment rules and scrutinise collaboration with Chinese universities. While the group asserted more influence in the Coalition joint party room than in Labor, MPs on both sides did everything they could to coordinate positions and ensure a broad bipartisanship on China.

They drew scorn from Gyngell and other veterans, including former ASIO and Defence department chief Dennis Richardson, who bridled at the way some Wolverines attacked their opponents. "For one group to continually wrap themselves in the flag and want to imply that those who disagree with them are not loyal Australians is simply crossing a line," Richardson told Sky News. "It's unacceptable, and they should be called out for that."

Gyngell also saw jejune sloganeering at the heart of the enterprise. "My objection was really to the alignment of one of the great policy dilemmas of our time with this Hollywood high-school fantasy of teenagers taking on a Russian invasion of America," Gyngell says. "The use of that sort of language, and that approach, trivialises and diminishes the issue, which is of really deep importance to Australia. And it diminishes Australian lawmakers... it's not simply a matter of turning a foreign policy issue into a meme."

That credo about the power of individuals ... seems to animate many of those who are currently winning the China debate

Paterson is dismissive here. He says the group's name was tongue-in-cheek and older critics of the Wolverines never really grasped how it was informed by a slightly online sense of pastiche and irony. He also argues the group was an "effective device for broadening the public conversation on China" and "attracting focus to the issue in a way that would be understandable to a wider audience".

"I think there is a very strong worldview among foreign policy elites that it is somehow grubby to seek democratic consent for foreign policy positions. I disagree," he tells me. "We could have just expressed concerns in highfalutin diplomatic language. And we would have been much less effective in achieving change if we had."

Either way, gauging the group's influence is no easy task. The Morrison and Turnbull governments have ticked off many items on the Wolverines' wish list, passing interference laws, creating a taskforce to combat meddling in universities, pressing for a COVID-19 inquiry, sharpening criticism of China's human rights record, blocking Huawei from the NBN, scrutinising and stopping several investment bids and tearing up the Victorian government's Belt and Road Initiative deal with Beijing.

Some members of the group believe the pressure they applied has been indispensable to this agenda. Other MPs scoff at that, saying the Wolverines did little but cheer on decisions which were always going to be made.

"They have timed their run very well," says one parliamentarian. "But they are also very good at taking credit for things where they were utterly peripheral."

The truth almost certainly lies in between. And in any case the Wolverines have now disbanded, with their most energetic members – including Paterson and Labor senator Kimberley Kitching – now ploughing their energies into the Inter-Parliamentary Alliance on China, which is trying to build international momentum for more forceful China policies within democracies. Policies that look much like Australia's.

Australia marches on

The question now is whether those policy settings are right. The federal government sees itself as ahead of the pack, staking out principled positions in Australia's interest and creating space for other states that are nervous at the prospect of a Chinese-led regional order to push back against Beijing's aggressive behaviour.

Some critics see Australia as hopelessly exposed and isolated, its relationship with its largest trading partner a smoking ruin, while other states, however friendly, desperately try to steer clear of the fracas.

Others have relatively few quarrels with the federal government's actual policies on China, but have criticised their implementation, suggesting the Coalition's language and tactics have often been clumsy and inflammatory. One former senior public servant told me he was "gobsmacked" that Foreign Minister Marise Payne had announced Australia would push for the COVID-19 inquiry before she'd rallied support from other countries. That same retired public servant also winced at recent attempts by the government to wring a political advantage from the China debate, including Dutton's accusation that Labor was "crab walking" away from the US alliance. "There is this unfortunate undertone that any attempt to resuscitate the diplomatic relationship or reset it is a betrayal or un-Australian," the former official tells me. "Yes, it must be on our terms, and, no, we can't give ground on core interests. But the idea that there are only two choices – fight on perpetually or collapse and surrender – is simply false."

Finally, there's the question of what happens if a military crisis starts to brew in the region. Australia may be a relatively marginal player in the looming flashpoints of the Indo-Pacific, but Dutton has already nailed this government's colours to the mast, declaring it was "inconceivable" Australia wouldn't back the United States in a war over Taiwan.

Hugh White – former senior Defence official and now Emeritus Professor of Strategic Studies at the Australian National University – sees current and emerging generations of analysts and politicians as bewilderingly nonchalant about the consequences of conflict, and the potential for catastrophic escalation. "One of the things that worries me is that in the decades since the end of the Cold War we have forgotten how important nuclear weapons are in these calculations," he told the ANU podcast *Democracy Sausage*. "People talk at length about the idea of a US–China war without ever mentioning they are both nuclear-armed states. For someone in my generation, my first decade in this business was the last decade of the Cold War, when we thought about nuclear weapons all the time. I keep on wanting to jump up and shake people and say, 'Remember what nuclear war means.'"

That argument draws a wry smile from Paterson, who says that critics cannot decide whether his generation is deliberately stoking the fires of war or is utterly oblivious to the risk of a conflagration. Either way, he is not for turning on China, and neither, it seems, is the Australian Government.

"I don't subscribe to historical inevitability. People and events can change the course of history," Paterson says.

He's talking about China's recent history rather than Australia's, and his belief that the global financial crisis, internal unrest in China and Xi's ascent allowed the hardliners to take control.

But that credo about the power of individuals to shape countries, and the power of countries to shape a region – despite the crushing forces of history – also seems to animate many of those who are currently winning the China debate in Australia today.

It's a gamble, and they're betting the house that they're right. ■

THE FIX
Solving Australia's foreign affairs challenges

—

William A. Stoltz on
How Australia could help
outlaw cyberweapons

"The timing is ripe for Australia to put practical measures like outlawing cyberweapons and standardising regulations at the heart of an international treaty on cybercrime"

THE PROBLEM: The international cyber domain is rapidly deteriorating into a disruptive, unregulated and unsafe environment for users, states and businesses. New technologies, new online marketplaces and digital currencies are combining to make it easier to build, buy and anonymously use increasingly damaging cyberweapons – or malware.

This has led to a global proliferation of "ransomware" attacks: the use of malware designed to hold hostage the data of computer networks until a ransom is paid. Indeed, ransomware attacks are now one of the most profitable forms of crime in the world. Victims, typically businesses, often pay up due to the urgent need to regain their data and the risk that refusing to pay, notifying authorities and spooking clients could lead to a hit to their share price greater than the cost of the ransom. Accordingly, regulators around the world have struggled to force businesses to report attacks and stop paying ransoms.

Furthermore, law enforcement agencies simply cannot detect or respond to every cyberattack, so states are increasingly reliant on businesses adopting best practice security measures. This includes actions like "patching" systems against known malware vulnerabilities, reporting cyberattacks, and cooperating with government agencies to mitigate vulnerabilities to critical infrastructure. However, there are no agreed standards for ensuring governments create consistent and appropriate regulations around these behaviours. For example, different jurisdictions have different rules about how quickly, how regularly and in what ways organisations should report cyberattacks and whether such reporting is made public. Also, as attacks become more persistent and sophisticated, businesses, particularly large firms, may be inclined to turn to the services of so-called "white hat" hackers and security firms that operate on the edge of the law, themselves potentially deploying malware to defend their clients. Such a shift would be a dangerous trend towards an even more lawless online environment, reminiscent of the company skirmishes of the Old West.

The volatility of the cyber domain is not being driven by criminals alone. There is also a wicked convergence between malicious state and non-state actors that is fuelling the spread of cyberweapons and increasing the risk of inter-state conflict. In early 2021, the Microsoft Exchange Server was subjected to a series of sophisticated cyberattacks, including ransomware, which affected approximately 250,000 servers worldwide and through them tens of thousands of organisations such as banks, parliaments and universities. In an unprecedented move, the member states of NATO, the EU and Five Eyes jointly denounced the attacks as being perpetrated by China's Ministry of State Security in collaboration with contract cybercriminals, such as the Hafnium hacker group.

Despite the urgent threat posed to international security by malware, possessing cyberweapons is not strictly a crime. Since the 1980s, legislation in most countries has focused on criminalising the harmful uses of malware, such as unauthorised access of a computer system, system damage or data theft. However, in Australia, the United States and the United Kingdom, and many other nations, it is not expressly illegal to *possess* malware. Allowing the possession of malware is counterintuitive when its use is illegal, and it places law enforcement and intelligence agencies in the unsustainable and ethically problematic position of being able to detect that someone has destructive cyberweapons but not able to intervene until they are used. It also means there is very little deterring criminals from purchasing or building malware and planning an attack.

THE PROPOSAL: Australia should advocate an international treaty to protect against cybercrime, with the criminalisation of malware and standardised regulations at its core.

The Australian government should initiate this campaign by instructing the Department of Foreign Affairs and Trade and the Department of Home Affairs to draft domestic laws to criminalise the possession of malware that can also be a model for other states to replicate. Criminalisation could resemble Australia's successful and internationally respected firearms controls. Australia could make it an offence for an individual to have malware on their computer, but could have sensible avenues for lawful, licensed possession, such as for academics who research cyberweapons or businesses that develop malware tools. DFAT could use the Australian legislation as the centrepiece for a diplomatic campaign to convince other states to draft their own laws and commit to an international treaty that outlines what constitutes malware and legitimate reasons for possession.

In the course of advocating for a malware treaty, Australia should also encourage the adoption of consistent international standards for preventing and responding to cyberattacks. These standards can be laid out in the treaty but will need to be codified in domestic regulations to have maximum effect. As compliance by businesses will be key, Australia could also convene dialogues between governments and transnational internet companies such as Microsoft, Alphabet Inc. and Amazon.

Cybercrime is a transnational problem, yet even common law countries have varied offences and penalties which can complicate joint international law enforcement investigations, prosecutions and extraditions of offenders.

WHY IT WILL WORK: Making something illegal doesn't make it go away, but in the case of cyberweapons it will raise the potential risks for criminals owning them and increase the cost for states allowing cybercrime to occur.

By their nature, cybercriminals are often hard to identify and many will remain anonymous. However, criminalising malware possession will have a deterrent effect by raising the potential costs of engaging in nefarious activities online.

Internationally consistent cybersecurity regulations would also clarify compliance for transnational companies and make it more obvious for governments, customers and investors around the world when a business is underperforming on cybersecurity best practice.

The treaty would put heightened international pressure on those states currently contracting cybercriminals. States such as China and Russia, which have leveraged cybercrime as part of their geostrategy, will be presented with a stark choice to either comply with the new international law and disavow such activities or refuse to engage and be regarded as cyber pariahs.

The United Nations is already exploring the potential scope and terms of a cyber treaty proposed by Russia. Western nations, including Australia and the United States, have resisted this treaty over concerns that Russia and other authoritarian states will use it to validate and entrench their policies of restricting how citizens can access and use the internet. However, in May 2021, after a vote of the General Assembly in favour of developing a cyber treaty in some form, the work of drafting it is now on the UN's agenda.

Australia is well placed to proactively shape its scope, especially as it is a vice-chair on the fifteen-member expert committee that will settle the terms for wider international negotiation. The timing is therefore ripe for Australia to put practical measures like outlawing cyberweapons and standardising regulations at the heart of an international treaty on cybercrime.

Despite the world being several decades into the digital age, cyber governance is still dangerously underdeveloped. As a digitally sophisticated democracy, Australia is well positioned to show the world how a safer digital society and international system can be achieved.

THE RESPONSE: The Department of Home Affairs agreed that international cooperation was crucial to acting against malware. However, it said the existing framework – known as the Budapest Convention – was adequate, stating that it allows "parties to develop their national legislation to criminalise cybercrime in a technology neutral manner" and "provides for procedural laws to support law enforcement to investigate and prosecute cybercrime, and facilitates international cooperation … for the collection of electronic evidence".

A spokesperson for the department said the federal government was amending legislation to make it an offence to purchase and sell malware. These changes were being introduced as part of the Australian Government Ransomware Action Plan, launched in October 2021. "Australia will continue to lead and build on the foundational principles established by the Budapest Convention to protect Australians and Australian businesses from the threat of malware and cybercriminals," the spokesperson said. ■

Reviews

***Dark Skies: Space
Expansionism,
Planetary Geopolitics
and the Ends of
Humanity***
Daniel Deudney
Oxford University Press

Until recently, spacefaring had seemed a spent horizon, not a fast-approaching future. After the 1986 *Challenger* disaster, even the US government lost faith in its own space evangelism, spearheaded so effectively by NASA during the Cold War. The Bush administration's decision to pull funding from national space programs to fund the war on terror marked the end of the first long cycle for the global space industry, a cycle dominated on the supply side by Boeing, Lockheed Martin and the old guard of defence contractors.

In the early 2000s, a cluster of Silicon Valley disruptors – Jeff Bezos and Elon Musk among them – joined with seasoned space lobbyists to begin picking apart the Boeing–Lockheed duopoly. The new space entrepreneurs were by then rich enough from dotcom capital to start heavily geared side projects, with the aim of buying their way into starring roles in the Cold War space fantasies of their boyhoods. It has taken nearly twenty years to get there. With their private fortunes reinforced by public contracts – many won through aggressive anti-trust litigation and legislative lobbying – both Musk's SpaceX and Bezos's Blue Origin have succeeded in developing reusable rocketry, the lynchpin of the next generation of spaceflight. In doing so, they have positioned SpaceX and Blue Origin as the duopoly providers for the space economy to come.

In that time, international space law has rebounded from near-total marginalisation in the 1990s to become a stage on which pandemic-era geopolitics is playing out. The new space race superficially resembles that of the Cold War, but there are crucial differences. In contrast to the bipolar days of old, more countries are developing independent spacefaring capacity. In the last five years, China, the European Space Agency and Israel have all conducted uncrewed lunar missions, and Japan and the United States have landed probes on asteroids. Others, led by Luxembourg and the United Arab Emirates, have positioned themselves as flagship jurisdictions for future aerospace activity. While Moon to Mars and asteroid programs grab headlines, the greatest increase in space traffic is far closer to Earth. A growing list of countries, including Argentina, Brazil and South Korea, are developing the capability to operate in geostationary orbit, 35,785 kilometres above the Earth's surface. So, too, are a horde of new aerospace corporations, Australia's Gilmour Space Technologies among them.

In other words, earth orbit is getting very, very busy; but where all this is leading, and why, receives far less policy consideration in Australia than it deserves. Space experts have long warned that increasing congestion will exacerbate longstanding regulatory problems, from dangerous space debris to grossly unequal access to geostationary orbit. In *Dark Skies*, Daniel Deudney argues that the biggest regulatory problem of all remains the one that birthed the field of air and space law in the late 1940s: the risk of nuclear war. Deudney, an international relations professor at Johns Hopkins University, challenges the pervasive belief that human expansion into space is both inevitable and inherently virtuous. Drawing on work in science and technology studies, history and literary studies, he maps out a sprawling ideology he calls "space expansionism". Within it, he identifies competing agendas: "military", "habitat" and "planetary security" priorities all vie for policy dominance. But fuelling all pro-space agendas is a hash of techno-utopian, libertarian and messianic ideals, bound together by a pseudo-religious belief that the existential threats faced by humanity on Earth will best be solved by leaving it.

Set aside the pro-space zeal, Deudney argues, and it becomes clear that the net results of applied aerospace technology have been equivocal at best; at worst, they have aggravated the risk of nuclear war. Despite the language of "peaceful exploration" written into legal and policy instruments at domestic and international levels, Deudney insists that aerospace technology is inextricable from its military origins. The danger is self-evident: a significant proportion of global military activity already takes place in low Earth orbit via satellite surveillance, and all spacefaring states save Japan have nuclear weapons. The United States, China, India and Russia have all flexed anti-satellite weapons (ASAT) capability over the last year, exploiting uncertainties in the framework of international space law. In November 2021, Russia tested ASAT weaponry on one of its defunct satellites, a dangerous act of geopolitical theatre that reportedly produced a debris field of over 1500 pieces.

Deudney concludes that if we are to avoid slouching towards a new age of mutually assured destruction, space programs the world over need to be scaled back urgently. Governments must agree to pursue programs compatible with an "Earth-centred pro-space agenda focused on nuclear and environmental security". Orbital weapons and ballistic missiles must be relinquished en masse, and plans for lunar and Martian colonisation abandoned. The existing multilateral Outer Space Treaty framework settled in the 1960s and 1970s – which permits the use of space for "peaceful purposes" only, prohibiting national appropriation and weaponisation – must be strengthened, and the use of space for Earth system science and astronomy expanded.

Dark Skies is a sprawling critique of popular thinking on space. Explorations of the darker motivations, gross inequalities and uncontrollable consequences of space activity are hardly new – sci-fi depends on them – but are habitually dismissed by space enthusiasts as anti-liberal or nihilistic. As such, Deudney's intervention is welcome, if only for emerging from the US international relations academy, usually a cheerleader for US military dominance. Moreover, a stripped-back, Earth-centred space agenda is, on the surface, a reasonable aspiration. But his solutions do little more than reiterate an ideal of international law as a mutually agreed restraint on sovereign power, calling for increased cooperation towards a comprehensive and stable space treaty regime. *Dark Skies* effectively lands us where we are now, once we escape the fumes of the space entrepreneurs: with a set of governance problems that have lurked on the global agenda for seventy years, and a beleaguered system of international diplomacy through which to address them.

Just a few short years ago, the new global space agenda was of peripheral concern in Australian policy circles. The Australian Space Agency (ASA) was established in Adelaide in 2018 within the Department of Industry, Innovation and Science, with a mandate of supporting the fledgling Australian aerospace industry to embed itself in revitalised US space-industry supply chains. As a result, the federal space agenda is largely being set by Australia's small but staunch and fast-organising industry – and the AUKUS alliance, with its emphasis on collaborative defence investment, has only underscored that commercial logic. The space industry wants to minimise bureaucratic obstacles to space operations, and to capitalise on the money pouring into the US sector. The ASA aims to attract increased foreign investment in Australian space companies, and to build a national industry involving 30,000 jobs with a $12-billion turnover by 2030.

But ad hoc reactivity to industry lobbying will not produce a mature national space policy, and is not a substitute for developing a strategic approach to an arena of international relations that is increasing in importance. In short, the ASA, with its commercial mandate, is an insufficient answer to the question of space. The capacity of the Department of Foreign Affairs and Trade to act within the shifting landscape of space diplomacy is vital. So, too, is a coherent defence policy that does more than fall in line with US imperatives. The unglamorous details of building trust, confidence and mutual endeavour over time – the core business of international diplomacy and lawmaking – are critical to Australia's long-term interests in space. While the entrepreneurs don their costumes, and Russia, China and the United States beat their chests, the United Nations, for all its flaws, still provides the most widely subscribed forum for negotiating new rules for space activity. Early in November 2021, the UN First Committee agreed to establish a working group to begin defining international norms for behaviour in space that mitigate the escalating risks of conflict. There will be hard work for Australian diplomats to do over the coming years, but DFAT has been starved of the resources required to maintain a strong diplomatic network, let alone in-house expertise on international space affairs.

Satellite surveillance and communications infrastructure now underpin the global economy. The notion that the commercial and military dimensions of foreign policy can be separated is as artificial in space as it is on Earth. Every Australian, along with everyone else on the planet, has a stake in space law and policy, whether the federal government acts to define and protect that stake or not. Deudney's title is misleading: if the crowding of Earth orbit continues, the one

thing the skies won't be is dark. SpaceX's Starlink division, a satellite internet service with plans for global coverage, intends to use every SpaceX flight to launch between sixty and 400 satellites into low-Earth orbit, with plans for up to 42,000 new satellites in the next few years. That we stand to lose the night sky to light pollution from a shroud of satellites and debris should itself be enough to send a shiver down the spine, even before we get to the risk of another nuclear age. Deudney's conclusion is ominous, and justifiably so: "soon we will no longer be protected from the consequences of our delusions by our incapacities, and we will suffer severely unless we learn to say no."

Cait Storr

Lion City: Singapore and the Invention of Modern Asia
Jeevan Vasagar
Hachette

Singapore presents a conundrum for Australian policymakers. A low-taxing, business-friendly city-state, it is now one of the richest nations in the world. Conservative think tanks consistently rate Singapore – where labour, capital and goods are able to move freely with minimal government intervention – as having the most "economic freedoms" in the world.

Yet dig a little deeper and Singapore's success quickly unsettles the neoliberal project. It is a state characterised by strong government and comprehensive provision of services, including near-universal government housing. Its world-leading educational success is driven by its government school system. Its economy has been shaped by an active industry policy, with government unafraid to identify and back emergent industries. And Singapore's taxes might be low, but its government generates quite a bit more revenue per person than Australia's, much of it non-tax revenue from state-owned enterprises.

Jeevan Vasagar's excellent book *Lion City: Singapore and the Invention of Modern Asia* explores this paradox, along with the many tensions that have shaped Singapore's development. No matter how you interpret Singapore's success, it is a nation of much interest to Australia. As a successful young nation with a heterogeneous population shaped by migration, it has many similar policy dilemmas to Australia. But it's richer than Australia, gets better educational outcomes and has longer life expectancy. And it has achieved all of this in just over fifty years, transitioning at warp speed from an impoverished tropical island with no natural resources.

Vasagar – former Singapore correspondent for the *Financial Times* – walks us through Singapore's history in lively fashion. His exploration is balanced; neither pro- nor anti-government. If anything, he fails to do justice to the sheer scale of Singaporean achievement. It is worth reflecting on. The World Economic Forum ranks Singapore number one on the Global Competitiveness Index (Australia is ranked sixteenth). The average fifteen-year-old Singaporean reads at a standard a year and a half ahead of their Australian counterpart; life expectancy is 83.6 years, higher than in Australia (83.4 years). Singapore has a negligible homicide rate (Australia's is five times higher; the rate in the United States is thirty-one times higher) and its GDP per capita of US$59,798 is quite a bit higher than Australia's (US$51,812). It's hard not to be impressed.

Characterised by technocratic competence and inscrutability, Singapore's government is a slick machine that sets out to learn from the world's best. Policies are rarely introduced without a comprehensive plan to implement them. And once implemented, they are changed sparingly, with a long-term view guiding the government's agenda.

This policy consistency is assisted by the stability that comes from never having had a change of government. While the Singaporean government maintains that it is "a fully democratic state", think tank Freedom House gives its democracy a score of 48 out of 100, labelling it only "partly free". Singapore's government has exhibited authoritarian tendencies, constraining the growth of opposition parties and limiting freedom of expression, assembly and association.

But could it be that this "pragmatic authoritarianism" is a fit-for-purpose style of government aligned with "Asian values"? The ruling People's Action Party justifies anti-democratic measures not as a means to hold onto power, but

as necessary for "holding together the common ground" – to stop the nation from fragmenting. Yet Vasagar argues that Singaporeans are not as conservative as their leaders make out. He reminds us that "Asian values" are not fixed but, rather, a political ideology constructed in the 1990s "to inoculate the population against the Western ideas that flowed in alongside Singapore's embrace of capitalism". The concept has been vigorously contested elsewhere in Asia, most notably by former Taiwanese leader Lee Teng-hui, who maintained that he had "faith in democracy and liberty" over a political system rooted in the Chinese dynastic system.

Singapore – like Australia – is torn between the United States, its major defence partner, and China, its major trading partner. This tension is amplified by the "Asian values" that the nation has been built on, aligning the country's culture more closely with China than the US. Its defence policy is shaped by the twofold doctrine articulated by Lee Kuan Yew in a 1966 speech: making itself a "poisonous shrimp" that would give a predator indigestion, or "swimming in the wake of a bigger fish". Consequently, Singapore has closely aligned with the United States while building up the most lavishly equipped armed forces in South-East Asia, modelled on – and advised by – the Israeli military.

A proudly multicultural nation, Singapore is made up of an ethnic Chinese majority, with sizeable Malay and Indian minorities. To accommodate this diversity and unify the nation, the government decided several decades ago that English would be the language of instruction in schools. English has since become the country's lingua franca: a fortuitous decision, allowing Singapore to serve as a global business hub in the heart of Asia.

Migrants now make up a large part of the island state's population – those from mainland China and elsewhere in Asia are relied on to do much of Singapore's dangerous, dirty or low-paid work. The living conditions of migrant workers were highlighted when major COVID-19 outbreaks spread through overcrowded dormitory accommodation. This catalysed a shift in sentiment towards greater community solidarity, with non-profit organisations raising funds for migrant workers and the government pledging to pay their healthcare bills.

Still, these migrants have no legal route to citizenship.

With one of the lowest birth rates in the world (at just 1.1 births per Singaporean woman) and among the longest life expectancy, Singapore is due to become one of the oldest nations in the world. Despite government efforts to encourage increased fertility through financial incentives and even state-sponsored match-making, the birth rate continues to decline, risking slower growth and a need for higher taxes to fund pensions. As in Australia, encouraging migration – with pathways to citizenship – is clearly part of the answer, but it "remains an intensely delicate subject".

Singapore's policy outcomes might be impressive, driven by technically capable leadership, but Vasagar points to a "gap in matters of the heart, soul and spirit" between the government and the people. One metric that Singapore does not do well in is happiness, scoring 6.4 out of 10 on the World Happiness Index published by the United Nations Sustainable Development Solutions Network.

While Singapore has built an impressive arts infrastructure in recent decades, Vasagar argues that "these gleaming new spaces lack new ideas to fill them". This buttoned-down nation "lacks a sense of fun". Yet there is increasing awareness that art plays a critical role, and that it's hard to be a global city without it. Censorship and restrictions are not particularly compatible with being a successful knowledge-based economy.

Ultimately, Vasagar is optimistic about Singapore's future: it has a strategically important location and is well governed; it is small and sovereign, allowing it to make difficult decisions more easily; and its people are highly educated, hard-working and fluent in English, as well as the most widely spoken languages in Asia. But Vasagar warns that "in the twenty-first century, [Singapore] must walk the line between populism and authoritarianism, allowing its people's voice to be heard". *Lion City* makes for great history, but importantly offers a nuanced and respectful examination of the forces and tensions that will shape Singapore's future "at the heart of Southeast Asia".

Andrew Wear

The American War in Afghanistan: A History
Carter Malkasian
Oxford University Press

n Herat, the beautiful, cultured and self-assured city in western Afghanistan, I watched members of a warlord's militia beat to death two men they accused of being Taliban, and throw their bodies into the street. Then they shot the remains full of bullets until one of them, at least, was unrecognisable. The killers punched the air with fists clutching guns and chanted *Allahu Akbar*, god is greatest.

I still carry the image of one young man, a walkie-talkie in his hand and an automatic weapon slung over his shoulder, turning to me from where he stood in the middle of the road near one of the red lumps that used to be a man, with a look on his face like a child just given an ice-cream cone. It seemed like one of the happiest moments of his life. He held the walkie-talkie to his mouth as he repeated the god-is-greatest mantra, letting clusters of militiamen elsewhere know of this micro-victory on the bridge at Ab Borda, a few kilometres from the city centre.

He was one of hundreds who had clustered around Ismail Khan, a seventy-two-year-old using the defence of Herat as a means of reviving his reputation as a warlord and warrior. A video of him dressed in white tunic and pantaloons, a signature black-and-white scarf around his head, jogging across the Pashtun Bridge ahead of his personal army had galvanised much of the country as it dealt with the fact that the Taliban were winning the war. The hope was that where the state's defence forces were failing, the warlords of yore could step in.

Ismail Khan's men had joined with armed members of the National Directorate of Security, the intelligence service, to hold the Taliban out of the city. The NDS men were professional soldiers, uniformed, well equipped, calm, focused. The best that could be said of the militias was that they were ragtag, excitable, fuelled by hope, adrenaline and bloodlust. This was what Herat had to offer. The army was nowhere to be seen, and there was no air support. As the young man with the walkie-talkie told me, it was one step forward and two steps back, day after day.

As the Taliban retreated, they left men embedded in the mostly empty houses and shops on the suburban outskirts of the city; these were snipers who fired on the republican forces and militias. That's how these two unfortunate men – both dressed in white, one with dark hair to his shoulders, the other cropped salt-and-pepper; apparently father and son – had been found, captured and dragged to their fate.

After dark fell on the evening of 2 August, the people of Herat took to their rooftops to chant *Allahu Akbar*. This was their way of reclaiming Islam, a religion that had been co-opted by the Taliban to justify a long, brutal and demoralising insurgency to retake control of Afghanistan. The next evening, in Kabul, and in other cities across the country, people marched through the streets chanting *Allahu Akbar*.

It was this nationwide cry of defiance that fixed in me the realisation that the Taliban had won the war. Twenty years of blood and brutality were ending, and Afghanistan's history of heartbreak and inhumanity was about to enter a new phase. It seemed that the words so central to their faith – to the identity of what often seems to be a country forsaken by God – were all the people had left to defend themselves.

Allahu Akbar: the chant of the insurgents as they committed atrocities against their fellow Afghans, soldiers and civilians, as well as the troops of foreign countries who had come to wreak revenge for the 9/11 attacks on the United States. The chant of child suicide bombers as they detonated explosive vests.

The Taliban initially said war would end with the expulsion of foreign forces. They moved the goal posts and said President Ashraf Ghani was the obstacle to peace, refused to agree to a ceasefire and kept on killing until Ghani fled in a helicopter to Uzbekistan on 15 August. The Americans leading the Western alliance said they wanted to keep the homeland safe: in that, at least, they were successful. Throughout the twenty-year engagement in Afghanistan, the United States did not suffer an atrocity like that of September 2001.

The American failures were not at home, they were in Afghanistan: the failure to include the Taliban in the post-2001 political settlement; to build up the Afghan security forces; to tackle official corruption; to admit the war was being lost.

I spent many years covering the war. As far as I can determine, I'm the only foreign journalist who was in Afghanistan when the Americans invaded on 7 October 2001, and again when the Americans turned the lights out at the Bagram air base near Kabul, which had been the hub of their war, and left in the dark of night.

Throughout those two decades, I do not recall ever being convinced that the war was anything but a cruel exercise in attrition. I interviewed generals and politicians, dined with ambassadors and charity bosses, and travelled with American and Afghan military to many parts of the country. I even spent four months working for a multilateral diplomatic mission. Some of the Afghan people I worked with remain close friends. Others sent me death threats. When I finally left Afghanistan on the last commercial flight from Kabul on

15 August before the Taliban entered the city, my overall impression was that Afghans were beset by cynicism. Everyone lied – about everything. Everyone knew they were lying and everyone knew they were being lied to. The fall of Kabul was only ever a matter of time. And everyone knew it. Anything else was one big cynical lie.

As the West's latest adventure in Afghanistan neared its denouement, coinciding with its twentieth anniversary, exhaustive accounts by authors and journalists eager to make their mark began to appear. Most saw the end approaching; it was only a question of how soon.

A few authors squeezed in last-minute changes and will no doubt update their second editions. It was easier for journalists like me, reporting from the frontlines, trying to get it right and knowing that what we got wrong today we could catch up on tomorrow. That said, no one reading my reports could have been in any doubt that the Afghan republic was crumbling. Had reality finally been prioritised over rhetoric in those final weeks, perhaps the chaos and tragedy that now define the end of the West's hubristic twenty-first-century adventure in Afghanistan could have been avoided.

The twentieth-anniversary books are a varied swag, ranging from the heartfelt and personal (*Afghan Napoleon* by Sandy Gall) to the action-packed (Wesley Anderson's *The Hardest Place*), the sharp punch of the fighting experience (*Walk in My Combat Boots* by Chris Mooney, James Patterson and Matt Eversmann), the detailed analysis (*The Afghanistan Papers* by Craig Whitlock) and the workaday and worthwhile (*The Longest War* by David Loyn).

Carter Malkasian's book is almost majestic, certainly authoritative, possibly definitive. A Pashtu-speaking historian and former adviser to US military commanders, Malkasian writes from the inside – not just from inside the Beltway but from Afghanistan itself. He knows the southern Pashtun heartland as few outsiders do, so his book is essential reading on how the American war in Afghanistan began, and why it was always fated to end the way it did.

Malkasian's previous book on Afghanistan, *War Comes to Garmser*, held a magnifying glass up to one district in one southern province. His latest book is more expanisve and yet offers explanations of Afghanistan's complex and complicated tribal anthropology, as well as the evolution of the Taliban, including the personality and thought process of its founding leader, Mullah Omar. What's more, Malkasian understands Hamid Karzai, the first president of the republic and a mercurial man central to America's relationship with Afghanistan.

America's war in Afghanistan was unwinnable. As Malkasian makes clear, the opportunity for peace was squandered when diplomacy was discarded. Along the way, the wrong people were empowered and enriched, and the population became embittered watching the corrupt thrive as they got poorer and hungrier. Now that the Taliban are back, the corruption, poverty and hunger are just as severe. The United States is no longer there to take the blame and, having departed, it no longer cares.

Ismail Khan, the warlord of western Afghanistan once known as the Lion of Herat, told me when I interviewed him on the frontline on 2 August that he saw the end coming. He pleaded for Afghanistan's neighbours to come to his country's rescue. The Taliban arrested him as they took Herat on 13 August and circulated a photograph of him in their custody. He is now living, quite comfortably it is said, in the Iranian city of Mashhad.

Lynne O'Donnell

Correspondence

"Pivot to India"
by Michael Wesley

Lavina Lee

Michael Wesley's article "Pivot to India?" (AFA13: *India Rising?*), shines a much-needed spotlight on the surprisingly underdeveloped relationship between Australia and India. Wesley carefully traces the trajectory of the relationship, from the estrangement of the Cold War era and the depths of discord after India's 1998 nuclear tests, to the relationship's recent peak in June 2020, when a Comprehensive Strategic Partnership between the two countries was declared.

Wesley offers some key insights into why both countries have neither valued each other nor understood each other's strategic culture, geopolitical anxieties and predicaments. India's historical experience as a subjugated rather than a privileged member of the British Empire gave rise to a post-independence worldview characterised by a high value for sovereign autonomy, an affinity with the 'have nots' of the global order and a reluctance to take on the mantle of great power status based on "might, coercion and exploitation". In contrast, Australia's Anglo-Saxon heritage and experience within the Empire allowed it to place trust and confidence in "great and powerful friends" – first Great Britain, then the United States – to "assuage its central anxiety – that it has too few people to defend such a large landmass".

That was then. Currently, Australia is dealing with a more economically and militarily powerful India that has the will to assert and defend its regional and global interests. The rise of an assertive and revisionist China, alongside the relative decline in US predominance in our region, has raised the hope and expectation that India will add to the strategic balance preventing Chinese dominance in the Indo-Pacific.

This leads to a central question in Wesley's article: will India emerge as a new "great and powerful friend" to Australia? While recognising that the two

Indian Ocean democracies have increasingly congruent views of China, Wesley warns Canberra against setting its expectations of India too high. Predictions of India's imminent rise to great-power status have indeed been proved wrong many times before. India's economic growth has been held back by poor institutions, a restrictive regulatory environment, a dysfunctional democracy and stubborn protectionist sentiments that have persisted since its socialist beginnings.

Wesley could have gone further in recognising other factors preventing India from playing a more robust role in balancing Chinese expansionism in our region. Compared to Australia, India is more vulnerable to Chinese retaliation and has less capacity to absorb punishment. The current border crisis in Ladakh demonstrates both India's susceptibility to Chinese salami-slicing tactics and how easy it would be for China to stretch Indian forces. Beijing could also encourage Pakistan to challenge to the Line of Control in Jammu and Kashmir. With a military budget almost four times smaller, and a nominal GDP one-sixth of China's, India is far more vulnerable to instability in its neighbourhood.

Further, while India has abandoned its formal commitment to "non-alignment", it retains a deep aversion to alliances and instead pursues "strategic autonomy" via multiple strategic partnerships. Wesley might have acknowledged the reality that this entrenched strategic culture precludes India from playing the role of security guarantor as our "great and powerful friends" have done in the past.

Nevertheless, it is still in Australia's interest to help India increase its material power on the basis that a stronger India will contribute to a more favourable strategic balance, regardless of whether the two countries are in alignment on all issues. India's recent enthusiasm for the Quadrilateral Security Dialogue shows its commitment to defending the rule of law, promoting quality infrastructure investment standards, partnering with advanced democracies in emerging technologies and becoming a trusted manufacturing hub and location for supply chains in critical sectors.

In the concluding section of his article, Wesley raises his most contentious arguments. He asserts that Washington has "ceded its pre-eminence in the Pacific" and "Australia will have to adapt to a multipolar regional order". For this reason, he argues, our "heliocentric perspective is a liability in a multipolar world".

The foundations for these assertions are not established. While US pre-dominance is in relative decline, it would be premature to conclude that we are entering a multipolar regional order "in which China and the United States become two among a series of great powers ... seeking to prevent any single state from dominating the region". The United States has not yet "ceded its pre-eminence in the Pacific" but has retained and reinvigorated its alliances and increased its forward presence.

Moreover, China might well be emerging as a regional peer competitor to the United States, but we are a long way from a regional order "in which China and the United States become two among a series of great powers", as Wesley asserts. For example, China spends more on its military each year than the combined military budgets of the whole of Asia and Oceania, and that gap is increasing. This is not suggestive of multipolarity. The iron law of numbers suggests that there can be no regional balance of power without the United States.

To be sure, deepening our relationship with India complements the overall objective of maintaining a favourable balance in the region. But with India's continuing limitations, Japan's military and demographic constraints, and Indonesia still some distance away from becoming a significant power, Australia has no choice but to enhance, encourage and support the US presence and power projection in our region and ensure that the United States remains our "great and powerful friend". The alternative would be to accept a regional order based on Chinese hegemony.

Lavina Lee is a senior lecturer in politics and international relations at Macquarie University and a member of the ASPI Council.

Ian Woolford

Facing uncertainty about current US foreign policy, and China's antagonism, Australia may be looking for a new "great and powerful friend". In his recent piece on the India–Australia relationship, Michael Wesley asks if that friend might be India. He charts the frosty origins of the relationship, identifies common characteristics and concludes that maritime security will be the most critical area of shared concern. Absent from Wesley's piece – save a mention of the willingness of Australia's conservative leaders to overlook Narendra Modi's "chauvinistic approach to communal relations at home" – is a critical discussion of the rise of Hindu nationalism. Though both countries have viewed this issue as an internal Indian matter, it has direct bearing on their relationship. This can be demonstrated by examining the three shared elements that Wesley lists as the backdrop for a natural partnership: democracy, diaspora and cricket. But first, an overview of Hindu nationalism, otherwise known as Hindutva.

The word "Hindutva" means something like Hindu-ness. But Hindutva is distinct from Hindu religious tradition. The term was coined by Vinayak Damodar Savarkar in 1923. He envisioned a Hindu nation in which Hindu identity was as much political as religious. In the Hindutva framework, Muslims are perpetual foreigners in India. If they are to stay, it is only through the goodwill of a Hindu majority. Hindutva is the founding principle of the Rashtriya Swayamsevak Sangh (RSS), a right-wing paramilitary organisation that formed in the 1920s. Early RSS leaders made no secret of their admiration for the fascists of Italy and Germany. M.S. Golwalkar, the second leader of the RSS, openly called for India to learn lessons about purifying the nation from Hitler. Through its relationship with the Bharatiya Janata Party (BJP), the RSS exerts immense influence over Indian politics. Modi himself rose through the RSS ranks, and Hindutva is a default position of the BJP under his leadership.

Wesley notes that the BJP came to power because the Congress Party was seen as "neglecting the Hindu majority to chase the votes of minorities". But the notion of a Hindu majority that speaks with a unified voice is fiction. It is a Hindutva talking point. It is why Hindutva ideologues bristle at discussion of diversity within Hindu tradition. They are especially troubled by critiques from India's feminists, Dalits, queers or other marginalised individuals. Those critiques lay bare the falsehood of a single Hindu voice. At its heart, Hindutva ideology is intellectually bankrupt. Its guiding principle is exclusion. When challenged, its proponents collapse into anti-Muslim blathering.

Wesley identifies commitment to democracy as a trait shared by India and Australia. But Hindutva is not compatible with democracy. Individuals who protest government action are labelled as "anti-national" and charged with sedition – especially those who protest the new Islamophobic citizenship law or show support for the ongoing farmers' protest. In the wake of the 2020 anti-Muslim violence in Delhi, police, instead of arresting perpetrators, targeted activists and academics known to speak up against Hindu nationalism. Several of my Indian academic colleagues are currently in prison and awaiting trial. As Hindutva rhetoric spreads, the environment has become increasingly deadly for journalists, academics and activists. Several high-profile individuals have been assassinated for their political views – including journalist Gauri Lankesh and university professor M.M. Kalburgi. This is not an internal Indian matter. It is a matter of international concern.

The Indian community in Australia is a second feature linking the two countries. Hindi is the eighth-most commonly spoken language in Australia, and Punjabi is Australia's fastest-growing language. Australia's Indian community is directly affected by the rise of Hindu nationalism. Reports recently surfaced that the Indian government revoked the Overseas Citizenship of India cards of several individuals in Canada after they joined rallies in support of Indian farmers. In addition to punishing overseas dissent, the Indian government has rewarded Indians who engage in violence to defend Hindu nationalism. Last year, Vishal Jood, an Indian national in Australia, pleaded guilty to charges of assault in connection to violent attacks against Sydney's Sikh community. Many of the protesting farmers in India are Sikh. Egged on by India's Hindu nationalist leaders, who stoke fears of minorities and label dissent as separatist and traitorous, Jood claimed that he was defending the nation and "the Tricolour" – that is, India's flag. High-level BJP officials, including the chief minister of Haryana, lobbied for Jood's release from prison. He was welcomed back to India with a parade and garlanded as a hero.

Wesley lists cricket as the third element of Australia's and India's shared tradition. Here, too, is an alarming trend. In October 2021, Pakistan defeated India in the men's T20 World Cup. Following the loss, individuals in multiple Indian states were arrested after being accused of celebrating Pakistan's victory. The office of Uttar Pradesh chief minister Yogi Adityanath, a Hindutva hardliner, gleefully tweeted out a headline: *"Pakistan ki jeet ka jashn manane valo par deshdroh lagega"* (Those celebrating Pakistan's win will be charged with sedition). These are new developments. Many still remember the 1999 Chennai test match, in which India was bested by Pakistan. The Indian crowd nevertheless gave a standing ovation to the opposing team. Even during a time of heightened tensions between India and Pakistan, mere months after India detonated nuclear warheads in Pokhran, India was not imprisoning citizens for cheering the wrong team.

Wesley identifies "America's lurch towards Trumpism" and the unpredictability of US foreign policy as causes of Australia's search for new powerful friends. If India emerges as such a friend, there will be good reasons to applaud. But the three pillars of Australia and India's shared tradition will collapse if human rights in India deteriorate further under Hindutva. Criticism of Hindutva – despite ideologues who label it "Hinduphobic" – should not be confused with criticism of Hinduism. Given the history of the India–Australia relationship, including the troubling role of the White Australia policy, Indians would be justified in viewing Australian talk of human rights abuses with suspicion. But Australia should not fall prey to a brand of racist Orientalism that views the new US authoritarianism as so shocking it requires a rethink of Australia's foreign policy, while seeing India's authoritarian turn as par for the course.

Ian Woolford is a lecturer in Hindi at La Trobe University.

Michael Wesley responds

Reading Lavina Lee's and Ian Woolford's comments on my essay prompted the thought that the rising prominence of India in the Australian geopolitical imagination is having a major positive consequence: the growing number of India specialists in our universities and think tanks. Whereas in the 1950s and 1960s Australia hosted some of the world's foremost Indianists, Indian studies went through a period of decline from the 1970s. That this is now being reversed is to be encouraged and celebrated.

Appropriately for such a big and diverse country, India is interpreted from a range of different perspectives. Lee and Woolford produce diametrically different takes on India, with very different implications for the evolving Australia–India relationship. Their perspectives are also very different from mine.

Lee has a pessimistic view of India's potential. She sees India as overshadowed by China, deeply vulnerable to its various forms of pressure on India. It is also vulnerable to regional instability, and the lingering influence of non-alignment renders it unable to engage in alliances that might bolster its power or security. Despite these disadvantages, Lee still believes Australia ought to help bolster India's material power in the interests of it contributing more to the Indo-Pacific's strategic balance. It's curious that she suggests that India's strategic culture precludes India from playing the role of Australia's security guarantor – this is precisely the central argument of my essay.

Lee disagrees with my suggestion that the Indo-Pacific is moving towards multipolarity, arguing that the United States maintains its strategic pre-eminence and that China is an emerging "peer competitor", and dismissing

India, Japan and Indonesia as actual or potential great powers. Her evidence for this is comparative GDPs and military spending. It is a mistake, in my view, to equate economic and military size with power. If it were this straightforward, the United States wouldn't have lost a war since 1945. It certainly wouldn't have been fought to a standstill by China during the Korean War, when China's economy and military capability were dwarfed by those of the United States.

My understanding of strategic affairs is that geography matters. That is why I spend so much time in my essay discussing geography and its impact on India's and Australia's strategic perceptions and judgements. The geography of the Indo-Pacific is arguably more important to the strategic balance than GDP or military spending. That is why US strategists concede that they can no longer be certain of prevailing in a war against China in the Western Pacific. It is the reason China is investing so heavily in reducing the vulnerability of its energy flows through the Indian Ocean. It is also why China has invested so heavily in its relationship with Pakistan since the 1960s – doing so keeps India off balance.

Factoring in geography means multipolarity is a more likely future than unipolarity or bipolarity. Japan, Indonesia and India loom large not because of their GDPs or military spending, but because of their locations. Each poses a potential threat to China's maritime approaches, an existential challenge for Beijing. And this is precisely why both Washington and Canberra are investing so heavily in relationships with them. If geography didn't matter, the Quad would make no sense.

Woolford's comment focuses on the Hindutva nationalism that animates the BJP government of India. This is certainly a concerning trend in Indian politics and communal relations, but Woolford struggles to make a case for why this is a significant factor in Australia–India relations. He will wait a long time before Australia makes human rights or democracy a central plank of its foreign policy. One of the most consistent elements in Australian foreign policy is a willingness to overlook a foreign regime's foibles if Australia has a strong interest in maintaining stable and positive relations.

The impact of Hindutva chauvinism on diaspora relations and cricket stretches credibility still further. I suggested these elements are helping to build the relationship, not that they are "pillars" of the relationship, as Woolford's reading has it. The central driving force in the burgeoning Indo–Australian relationship is geopolitics. With the deepening of strategic rivalries in the Indo-Pacific in the years ahead, it is highly unlikely that the ideology of either government will factor significantly in the relationship.

Michael Wesley is Deputy Vice-Chancellor International
at the University of Melbourne.

"The Fix"
by Elizabeth Buchanan

Bob Brown

Canberra's twenty-year action plan for Antarctica aims to "minimise the environmental impact of Australia's activities". The arrival of the new Antarctic ship *Nuyina* (noy-yee-nah) in Hobart last October met that aim.

Built in Romania and fitted out in the Netherlands, *Nuyina* is "the world's most advanced Antarctic icebreaker, science and resupply ship". It is 160 metres long, 50 metres tall, painted bright orange and almost silent. The ship cost $529 million, and the Australian government has committed $1.9 billion to its operation over the next thirty years.

According to Sussan Ley, Minister for the Environment, "RSV *Nuyina* will soon be the backbone of the Australian Antarctic Program. It will establish a scientific legacy that will last for generations."

On the day of the vessel's arrival in Hobart, Prime Minister Scott Morrison noted that, since the time of Sir Douglas Mawson, Australia has "led the way in the care, protection and understanding of Antarctica … one of the planet's greatest treasures".

Nevertheless, in 2018, Morrison flagged a much bigger commitment to building a concrete airport near Australia's Davis Station in Antarctica – one that would not "minimise" Australia's environmental impact.

The multibillion-dollar 2700-metre runway, capable of handling Boeing 787 Dreamliners and RAAF Boeing C-17A Globemasters, would require more than 3 million cubic metres of earthworks and the transport from Australia of 115,000 tonnes of concrete pavers.

Sixty vertical metres of the Vestfold Hills would be levelled, using explosives. Nearby Adélie penguin and Weddell seal breeding colonies would face displacement. A lake would be destroyed.

The infrastructure would include a taxiway, aircraft apron, runway lighting and buildings for services such as air traffic, rescue and firefighting.

The Australian Antarctic Division considered building a runway in the Vestfold Hills in the 1980s, 1990s and 2000s, but it abandoned the idea each time because of the immense environmental impacts involved. Ski-fitted aircraft, using ice runways, were a more flexible aerial alternative.

According to the US aviation news service AeroTime, in addition to increased air connectivity, "another argument for the new aerodrome is Australia's strategic concerns to counter China's growing presence in Antarctica".

In "The Fix" (AFA13: *India Rising?*), Elizabeth Buchanan agrees: "In theory, the case for developing the runway is essentially benign … but in practice, the Davis runway would be a strategic asset for Australia. It would afford Canberra quick unfettered access to the continent on our southern flank'.

The practical reason for developing the runway is strategic: to create just the menace that the 1959 Antarctic Treaty was meant to avoid.

This boiled down to Australia – a time-honoured leader in keeping Antarctica a global environmental asset, free of commercial and military competition – getting ready to set off a race for strategic control of the continent.

Even if Australia were to offer free and unfettered use of the airport to China, Russia, India and all other nations, how could an Australian concrete runway not give others licence to build their own?

Australia would be offering the perfect excuse for the long-dreaded age of Antarctic commercial and militaristic exploitation, which the Antarctic Treaty, the 1980 Convention on the Conservation of Antarctic Marine Living Resources and the 1998 Madrid Protocol, prohibiting mining, specifically aimed to prevent.

Buchanan notes that China has plans to build an Antarctic runway of its own at nearby Zhongshan Station (though these plans were stalled, "with Beijing employing a 'wait and see' approach to the Vestfold Hills site. Why build on a sub-par site when the best site might remain vacant?"). Like all other airstrips in Antarctica, Zhongshan would be on the ice.

Morrison's proposed runway was in line with the view of Antarctica expressed by Deputy Prime Minister Barnaby Joyce after he visited Casey Station in 2006: "There's minerals there, there's gold, there's iron ore, there's coal, there's huge fish resources and what you have to ask is: 'Do I turn my head and allow another country to exploit my resource ... or do I position myself in such a way as I'm going to exploit it myself before they get there.'"

Joyce's words increased the fears of many of Australia's Antarctic scientists, who saw a concrete Davis airport as environmental desecration, if not a Trojan horse for exploitation.

They were therefore delighted at the arrival of the *Nuyina* in Hobart. Here was the perfect next step for facilitating Australia's historic lead in peaceful scientific research in Antarctica – not least research into the impacts of global warming on the continent, and their flow-on to the rest of the planet.

Three decades ago, the French ship *L'Astrolabe* docked in Hobart, loaded with explosives and bulldozers to build a runway at its Antarctic Dumont d'Urville Station. This involved blowing up Adélie penguin rookeries. Environmentalists hung a giant banner opposite *L'Astrolabe* reading "NON!", and two stowed away on the ship to complicate its progress. In the event, a winter storm smashed the French runway preparations.

If the Morrison government had purloined *Nuyina* to transfer 10-tonne concrete pavers rather than scientific personnel and equipment to Davis – and that was its plan – there would have been more than banners out to say "NO!" once again.

But on 25 November, after a short but effective public campaign, Minister Ley announced that the government had canned the airport proposal near its Davis base.

Australia was back on track as conservator, rather than concreter, of Antarctica.

Bob Brown is a former parliamentary leader of the Australian Greens.

Donald R. Rothwell

A ustralia is a major Antarctic power. Australian explorers, scientists, expeditioners and tourists have been travelling to Antarctica for over a century. Australia's claim to the Australian Antarctic Territory – extending to 42 per cent of the continent – is the largest of the seven territorial claims on the continent. Australia was an original party to the 1959 Antarctic Treaty and in 1961 hosted the first formal treaty meeting in Canberra. The Hawke government promoted an international pivot away from an Antarctic minerals regime in favour of environmental protection. The result was the 1991 Madrid Protocol, prohibiting mining and establishing a comprehensive environmental management regime. Australia has three research stations on the continent, at Casey, Davis and Mawson, which operate year round. The importance Australia attaches to promoting Antarctic science was highlighted in 2021 by the arrival in Hobart of Australia's new $529-million Antarctic icebreaker, RSV *Nuyina*.

This backstory, its associated legacies and its contemporary interests are often overlooked in Canberra and the wider community. They provide some context to the government's November 2021 decision to abandon the Davis aerodrome project.

Australian Antarctic policy, which has enjoyed bipartisan support, is founded on three pillars: support for Australia's claim to its Antarctic territory, support for the Treaty system and support for Antarctic science. Australia has also practised deft Antarctic diplomacy, including advancing claims to an extended Australian continental shelf in the Southern Ocean from the sub-Antarctic Heard and McDonald Islands, and challenging Japan's Antarctic whaling in the UN International Court of Justice. The prime example of this diplomacy is the Hawke government's promotion of the Madrid Protocol, which created an ongoing legacy for Australia and Antarctica. The result is that Australia's Antarctic environmental credentials are impeccable.

In "The Fix", Elizabeth Buchanan rightly highlights the geopolitical issues that currently swirl around the Antarctic. Interest in Antarctica has increased considerably in recent decades. While membership of the Antarctic Treaty appears static, scientific engagement is growing. This is partly due to climate change, which is making Antarctica more accessible, and also a more strategic location for climate research. China's growing interest in polar affairs – it has strong engagement in the Arctic as a growing maritime power and observer on the Arctic Council – should not be underestimated. While not an original Antarctic Treaty party, China has now adopted all of the key instruments and is a very active player in Antarctic law, policy and politics.

There can be no denying that the Davis aerodrome project could have been a game changer for Australia in Antarctica. It would have opened up opportunities for Australian science that previously were only dreamed of, and it would have significantly expanded Australia's presence in the Australian Antarctic Territory. The importance of Australia being physically present in Antarctica should not be overlooked. Australia's Antarctic claim is not settled. The Antarctic Treaty effectively neutralises territorial claims. That has not stopped others from positioning themselves to stake a claim if one day the treaty comes to an end. The Davis aerodrome project would only have enhanced Australia's territorial claims. It would have sent a very strong signal to others about Australia's intentions.

Ultimately, however, the Morrison government determined that the project was not feasible on the grounds of environmental impact and cost. Balancing science, the environment, budget, Australian interests and Antarctic geopolitics was always going to be a challenge. The Madrid Protocol would have required a comprehensive environmental evaluation prior to progressing the proposal to debate at the annual Antarctic Treaty meetings. The domestic politics would also have needed careful management. Tough questions could have been posed during the 2022 federal election over the Coalition's Antarctic environmental credentials. In the wake of the 2021 Glasgow climate summit debates over Australia's Paris Agreement commitments, abandoning the aerodrome allows the government to sidestep that environmental spotlight.

There is every prospect that other powerful Antarctic players may now seek to take advantage of Australia abandoning the aerodrome project. Madrid Protocol procedures will, however, also apply to them. Environment minister Sussan Ley alluded to this in the government's 25 November press release, which observed, "All nations need to place the Antarctic environment at the absolute centre of decision-making and respect the treaty system." Australia will no doubt point to its principled position in promoting Antarctic environmental protection through the Madrid Protocol and now its abandonment of the aerodrome project. The Morrison government is building on the Hawke government's legacy in this regard. The challenge ahead will be to continue to promote protection of the Antarctic environment in the face of climate threats and geopolitical challenges.

Donald R. Rothwell is a professor of international law at the ANU College of Law, and a specialist in polar law.

Elizabeth Buchanan responds

n AFA13: *India Rising?*, I tabled the strategic logic behind securing year-round aviation access to East Antarctica – where the majority of Australia's 42 per cent claim to Antarctica lies. The Morrison government's decision not to proceed with the Davis aerodrome project (DAP) is not merely an opportunity lost. It is a confirmation that Australia has no Antarctic strategy.

Bob Brown correctly highlights Australia's important environmental and scientific legacies in Antarctica. Given the persistence with which various runway projects crop up in the Australian Antarctic Division (at least every decade or so), one could argue that the environmental concerns are well established. Yet environmental protection is merely one of many interests Australia must balance in Antarctica.

Indeed, as Brown notes, I believe the runway would have been a strategic asset for Australia. Brown labels strategic competition as "just the menace" the Antarctic Treaty sought to avoid. However, the treaty itself is a *tool* of strategic competition, chiselled by Cold War contestation. The idea that Australia's Davis runway would "set off a race for strategic control of the continent" is a popular one. This betrays a narrow assumption about *just what* strategic control looks like at the South Pole.

Chinese boots on the ground and Moscow's annexation of the area around Vostok Station aren't likely. Yet Chinese-controlled scientific research or Chinese nationals completing sensitive research in Australia and returning home with the intellectual property are certainly elements of strategic competition on the ice.

Like Brown, many argue the runway would have been "the perfect excuse for the long-dreaded age of Antarctic commercial and militaristic exploitation".

However, any exploration of resources today is deemed permissible if slapped with the "scientific" label. Tourism is proliferating. A private firm recently landed an Airbus A340 on the continent for the first time – the first of many flights ushering in a new age of hyper-human activity in Antarctica.

Perhaps, on closer inspection, Australia's environmental legacy argument is dirtier than it seems. Bob Hawke did lead Australia's role in prohibiting Antarctic mining via the 1998 Protocol on Environmental Protection to the Antarctic Treaty (the Madrid Protocol). However, the Hawke government's original policy setting was more aligned with the Convention on the Regulation of Antarctic Mineral Resource Activities (CRAMRA), under which mining would have been permitted but regulated closely. Australia sunk CRAMRA in final negotiations, paving the way for the Madrid Protocol, due to disputes over economic dividends. If Australia wasn't going to reap the economic rewards of 42 per cent of the riches mined, then no one would.

The Bob Brown Foundation ran a "short but effective" campaign in response to the runway project. The foundation's press release celebrating the termination of DAP noted that "Antarctica is facing unprecedented threats due to climate change, fishing pressures and tourism". Of course, the runway could have facilitated the management and understanding of these challenges via a bolstered logistical capability.

Don Rothwell rightly expresses some dismay at Australia's decision to walk away from the project. I agree that an Australian presence is a necessary precursor to *protecting* Antarctica. Australia has some of the world's highest environmental standards when it comes to Antarctic infrastructure, and Canberra respects the treaty mechanisms. This cannot be stated of many of the other Antarctic players.

Presence is also an important mechanism for future-proofing Australia's Antarctic legacy. As Rothwell notes: "Australia's claim is not settled." This fact should be at the forefront of Canberra's Antarctic strategy – driving our leadership within the Antarctic Treaty System (which it is in our interest to preserve) while maintaining a clear position in the Australian Antarctic Territory.

Of course, Canberra still needs to secure year-round aviation access to Antarctica. Yet the tabled solutions are fraught with risk. Environment minister Sussan Ley has noted that access will be facilitated via helicopter from Australia's new icebreaker *Nuyina*. But this vessel is still to undergo final ice-sea trials. Furthermore, the reliance on a *single* vessel assumes Antarctic emergencies or strategic challenges will wait until the vessel is in proximity to the continent.

Ley's point that "all nations must…respect the treaty" overlooks the uncomfortable reality that every state interprets the treaty differently. As is the nature of international law, domestic conceptions of "respect" differ. The Australian government appears to have taken a "principled position" when it comes to DAP. Meanwhile, private tourist operators book more flights to Antarctica, building their own runways. Perhaps hotels are next? States such as Italy have built new gravel runways to reduce aviation dependence on the United States. Renewed efforts to secure access to Antarctica are also evident in increased scoping for port development across the continent. Australia is well and truly on its way to watching from the sidelines (albeit with its "principled position").

Perhaps DAP will be revived in another decade, given that year-round aviation projects tend to reincarnate. Of course, one wonders if the cost hurdle and environmental grounds cited are simply a ruse to scare off other states from scoping similar infrastructure. Costs could have been mitigated via international partnerships and collaboration. DAP was scrapped before the know-how to build a concrete runway in Antarctica was shared. Could we have innovated a cheaper alternative?

If Canberra built the runway, we'd require capability to utilise it (and, perhaps, to *defend* it) – and that would require strategic foresight and a decadal vision of security interests. Things Australia doesn't currently appear to have.

Elizabeth Buchanan is a lecturer in strategic studies at Deakin University and a fellow of the Modern War Institute at West Point Military Academy.

Subscribe to Australian Foreign Affairs & save up to 28% on the cover price.

Enjoy free home delivery of the print edition and full digital as well as ebook access to the journal via the Australian Foreign Affairs website, iPad, iPhone and Android apps.

Forthcoming issue:
Our Unstable Neighbourhood
(July 2022)

Never miss an issue. Subscribe and save.

☐ **1 year auto-renewing print and digital subscription** (3 issues) $49.99 within Australia. Outside Australia $79.99*.

☐ **1 year print and digital subscription** (3 issues) $59.99 within Australia. Outside Australia $99.99.

☐ **1 year auto-renewing digital subscription** (3 issues) $29.99.*

☐ **2 year print and digital subscription** (6 issues) $114.99 within Australia.

☐ Tick here to commence subscription with the current issue.

Give an inspired gift. Subscribe a friend.

☐ **1 year print and digital gift subscription** (3 issues) $59.99 within Australia. Outside Australia $99.99.

☐ **1 year digital-only gift subscription** (3 issues) $29.99.

☐ **2 year print and digital gift subscription** (6 issues) $114.99 within Australia.

☐ Tick here to commence subscription with the current issue.

ALL PRICES INCLUDE GST, POSTAGE AND HANDLING.

*Your subscription will automatically renew until you notify us to stop. Prior to the end of your subscription period, we will send you a reminder notice.

Please turn over for subscription order form, or subscribe online at **australianforeignaffairs.com**
Alternatively, call 1800 077 514 or +61 3 9486 0288 or email **subscribe@australianforeignaffairs.com**

Back Issues

ALL PRICES INCLUDE GST, POSTAGE AND HANDLING.

- ☐ **AFA1** ($15.99)
  The Big Picture
- ☐ **AFA2** ($15.99)
  Trump in Asia
- ☐ **AFA3** ($15.99)
  Australia & Indonesia
- ☐ **AFA4** ($15.99)
  Defending Australia
- ☐ **AFA5** ($15.99)
  Are We Asian Yet?
- ☐ **AFA6** ($15.99)
  Our Sphere of Influence
- ☐ **AFA7** ($15.99)
  China Dependence
- ☐ **AFA8** ($15.99)
  Can We Trust America?
- ☐ **AFA9** ($15.99)
  Spy vs Spy
- ☐ **AFA10** ($15.99)
  Friends, Allies and Enemies
- ☐ **AFA11** ($15.99)
  The March of Autocracy
- ☐ **AFA12** ($22.99)
  Feeling the Heat
- ☐ **AFA13** ($22.99)
  India Rising?

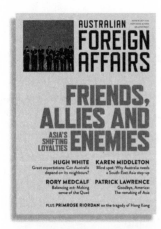
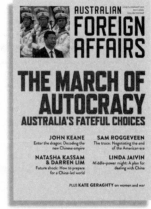
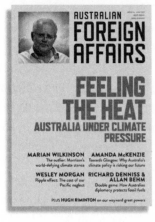
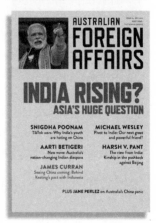

PAYMENT DETAILS I enclose a cheque/money order made out to Schwartz Books Pty Ltd. Or please debit my credit card (MasterCard, Visa or Amex accepted).

CARD NO.

EXPIRY DATE   /   CCV   AMOUNT $

CARDHOLDER'S NAME

SIGNATURE

NAME

ADDRESS

EMAIL   PHONE

Post or fax this form to: Reply Paid 90094, Collingwood VIC 3066 **Freecall:** 1800 077 514 **or** +61 3 9486 0288
Fax: (03) 9011 6106 **Email:** subscribe@australianforeignaffairs.com **Website:** australianforeignaffairs.com
Subscribe online at australianforeignaffairs.com/subscribe (please do not send electronic scans of this form)

FOREIGN POLICY CONCEPTS AND JARGON, EXPLAINED

BLADDER DIPLOMACY

What is it: A diplomatic ploy that merits an entry in *Brewer's Dictionary of Phrase & Fable*: "the tactic of assaulting one's diplomatic adversary's bladder with large quantities of liquid".

Who coined it: The phrase has been in use since at least the 1960s, but was made famous by James Baker III (former secretary of state, United States). He went up against the bladder diplomacy world champion, Hafez al-Assad (former dictator, Syria), whose iron-willed toileting endurance has become legend. In one marathon session, he remained seated for nine hours and forty-five minutes, until Baker finally waved a "white handkerchief" for a break.

Could it be countered: Baker tipped off one of his successors, Madeleine Albright (former secretary of state, United States), and she politely declined al-Assad's array of lemonade, water and Turkish coffee. Ronald Reagan (former president, United States) earlier learnt to avoid drinking coffee while negotiating; instead, he would mime sips, before throwing the beverage into a potted plant.

Where else has it been used: During negotiations for the Iran nuclear deal in 2015, which lasted so long attendees marked the duration by how many changes of shirt they required.

Does it work: Sometimes. Henry Kissinger (former secretary of state, United States) claimed that during arms negotiations, Richard Nixon (former president, United States) made concessions because the Soviets refused to tell him where the men's room was.